MEGA
Creativity

*How to Solve Problems,
Make Art, and Change Your World*

JOHN BOTHA

ISBN: 978-1-0492-7623-6 (ebook)
ISBN: 978-1-0492-7622-9 (print paperback)

Self-published by John Botha
First edition
Published in 2026

For permissions inquiries, please contact the author.

For Samantha

CONTENTS

INTRODUCTION

In April 2020, the world stopped. I remember driving along the main roads of Cape Town. It was rush hour, and I was the only car on the road. The traffic lights flashed colours to an empty street, coordinating invisible traffic. Wildlife appeared on the roads. I could drive as fast or slow as I liked, and there was no one to complain.

The COVID-19 pandemic was spreading. Governments mandated lockdowns, we isolated, and most of us were left to news updates and our own nervous thoughts. We questioned our futures, our mortality, our connection to each other, and our purpose. I started writing.

At first, my writing was not about creativity at all. I had time and space to write about anything, often blogging online to pass the pandemic hours. But the more I wrote, the more I was drawn to the concept of creativity and the creative process. I developed a core insight: our creativity shapes everything.

A grand picture formed—one where creativity connects all people and fields. Soon, creativity became my driving interest and an endless source of ideas—the phases, feats, and facilitation of creativity. I realised creativity happens not only on the grand scale, where figures like Einstein and The Beatles transform their fields and delight millions, but also on the personal scale with daily acts that form your home and family life. I became interested in all types of creativity, because the creative process is a universal constant across our culture and affairs.

This book has a COVID origin story, but I've always been fascinated by the threads that connect our culture. As an actuary working in healthcare, I do not operate in a traditionally creative domain like art or music—but I reject the idea that my work is any less creative. It's precisely this perspective that drove me to understand creativity in a deeper way.

My original insight, and the core of this book, is a new framework to help you think about the creative process and apply it to any kind of problem or project. This MEGA model can help you rethink the role of creativity in your life by organising and inspiring your creative work.

We've lost a wider and deeper understanding of creativity that needs to be reclaimed. I have researched creative frameworks, great works and people, the psychology of creativity, the way culture evolves, and how ordinary people change the world by applying the creative process well. The result is this book. It's a guide for creative work.

If you don't think you're creative: I will show you why you are and how you can be creative in ways that might surprise you. For those of you who are comfortable in your creativity, I will offer a framework that makes the process more practical.

Many people view creativity as mystical—an angel guiding the brush, a muse whispering through the strings. There *is* something magical about creativity, but the magic comes from a process, accessible to every creative human who attempts to channel their talents and experiences.

The first law of MEGA creativity: *Every person is creative.*
The second law: *Every field is creative.*

It does not matter what you work on; the capacity to be creative is practically endless in every domain.

What Is Creativity?

John Cleese calls creativity "a way of operating," and *MEGA Creativity* builds on this practical philosophy.

Creativity is the way we usher in the music, stories, explanations, technologies, and ideas that reshape our world. We have an innate ability to solve problems in any context. The late Sir Ken Robinson said that creativity is a *process of getting to new ideas that add value*. A process. New ideas. Value. This book unpacks this magnificent process.

The philosopher Karl Popper claimed that *all life is problem-solving*. Creativity is at the centre of living—both problem-solving and expression. It is a serious and far-reaching topic, more than most realise. Creativity is an inherently human capacity—the key to our success as a species, the engine of progress in any domain and in any way of life. Humans wield creativity to evolve culture: innovating economies, birthing art, furthering science, and expanding our conception of the world and our place within it. Creativity is for these grand pursuits and for the small acts of daily living. Embracing creativity expands our view of what is possible.

To explore all of these ideas, this book is structured in three parts:

Part 1 (MEGA Phases) expands on the four high-level phases of the creative process—Motivation, Exploration, Generation, Amelioration—captured collectively with the acronym MEGA:

- **Motivation** is problem selection—guided by unique curiosity, talent, and purpose.
- **Exploration** is problem framing and learning—by seeking knowledge and skills.
- **Generation** is producing new ideas—with recombination and experimentation.
- **Amelioration** is solution shaping—refining, evaluating, and sharing your work.

Part 2 (MEGA Tools) looks at how you can become more creative (across MEGA phases):

- In **Psychology**, we look at the mindset required for creativity, and the traits of highly creative people.
- In **Practices**, we talk about the when, where, how, and who of a sustained creative practice.
- In **Protocols**, we look at four approaches to refresh creative work: framing constraints, switching phases, shifting perspective, and keeping momentum.

Part 3 (MEGA Living) looks at why creativity matters. Specifically, we focus on how agency, value creation, and greater creative engagement enrich your life.

How to Read This Book

You can jump to any section that is most relevant to your creative work right now. The creative process is not linear, so you'll want to zig and zag through different phases. MEGA phases happen in parallel. All phases are always running in your subconscious, but you can learn to focus on one at a time to make progress. If you want new ways to think about doing research, then you can start with chapter 2, "Exploration." Or, if you're looking for practical ideas about how to systematise creative work, chapter 6, "Practices" may be relevant. Go to chapter 3, "Generation," if you seek new ideas. Be selective in your reading.

Who Is This Book For?

This book is for anyone looking to better understand their creative potential—how to focus their fantastic faculties and how to build more creative practices. *MEGA Creativity* is a framework for instilling energy, agency, and structure. This book is for ordinary and extraordinary acts. It's for:

- artists looking for practical advice on systematising creativity
- leaders and teams looking for more interesting ways to work together and innovate

- parents seeking ways to build experiences for their family
- entrepreneurs thinking about value creation
- scientists looking for original ideas
- educators and students looking to bring learning to life
- young people figuring out what they want from their work
- anyone looking for more engagement in their work or seeking a more connected and fulfilling life

The MEGA Approach

MEGA Creativity is an extensive framework. You need not consume it whole; you can carve off the bits that work for you.

We'll consider phases, protocols, and practices that can help lift you to new creative heights—but we'll also see why this is relevant to everyday creativity, achievable by anyone. We might all aspire to do great work, but there are so many layers of creativity that can improve our lives before greatness. More often it's simply about embracing the creative life: by solving small problems and writing the script of your day with a more heightened sense of agency.

As artificial intelligence takes off in the twenty-first century and we question what work is relevant for the future, understanding creativity has never been more important. *MEGA Creativity* is a framework for human flourishing. Creativity is the engine of personal and cultural evolution. Individuals solve problems to build new cultural capital. Hence, creativity gives us the power to change the world. Just as genetic mutation is the mechanism for biological evolution, creativity shapes culture.

Creativity can both build and destroy. Our creative minds make us tremendously powerful. We should all be more excited about our capacities for personal and collective creativity; our lives and futures depend on it.

In this book I will show you a doorway. Behind this door is light and warmth, a view of life infused with creativity and possibility. Steal a glimpse at the brilliant colour on the other side. Take the first step through.

PART 1:
MEGA PHASES

A new look at the creative process.

CHAPTER 1: MOTIVATION

Be Weird – Creative Domains – The Curiosity Bull's-eye – Many Motives

All life is problem solving.

—Karl Popper

Don't ask yourself what the world needs. Ask yourself what makes you come alive, and go and do that. Because what the world really needs is more of us to come alive.

—Howard Thurman

Motivation is the colour green; the signal to go. The first of the four phases of MEGA Creativity is motivation. It's the most overlooked phase: the starting line few talk about. Motivation is the hard work of choosing creative projects that you care about.

The question of *why* simmers beneath everything. Motivation asks "why" questions. These questions are difficult because they ask us to confront ourselves honestly. Motivation provides the flaming match that illuminates and sparks your next move. Selecting the right problems is the most crucial application of creativity. Interrogating motivation will steer you towards the creative engagements that are most suited to you—both the projects for your career and the activities that make your life richer.

You discover what you like doing by trying things. Your motivation, and your potential, is revealed with action. Motivation is a phase you will return to often. The work of finding new problems and staying inspired is no trivial matter. Creative projects can be hazy and daunting but beginning them need not be. It starts by asking why the work matters to you, and letting the rest follow.

In this chapter, we will look at the many edges of motivation. We begin by asking what it means to be weird and why you must embrace your unique point of view. We look at creativity as problem-solving, with problem selection as the first phase. We discuss the many kinds of creative domains (across arts, science, business, and life), and stress the importance of aligning creative work to curiosity, talent, and purpose. Lastly, we consider the motives that sustain a creative life and the motives that mislead.

Be Weird

Always stick to what makes you weird, odd, strange, different. That's your source of power.

—Robert Greene

Motivation is the key to open creativity, but each lock is different. Motivation starts with you. There is no one else like you—every person is utterly unique. This is a statistical, biological, incontrovertible fact. Genetics, life experiences, cultural shaping—we are each born and programmed differently. This endows each of us with something special, something different. Creativity is the way we cultivate this difference.

Matters of motivation must be seen in this light. Only you can figure out what attracts and engages your creativity. Your engine of motivation is singular, so let it drive you to interesting places. The way you see the world is unique. The secret to a meaningful life is believing that you have something special and worthwhile to share. This is the ultimate source of motivation: when you realise your contribution can have value and that your creativity is the way to its realisation.

Without honest interrogation of motivation, people live according to the scripts of others. For a while this chase might distract you—but you will soon find it is not enough. Work without creativity is like air without oxygen. The creative life is part of the good life: how you spend your time matters; the work you do matters. It's imperative you spend some time thinking about this.

The cultivation of your interests and preferences—your weirdness—takes a great deal of work. Individuals build out unique perspectives by following their tastes and talents over time. Knowing you are different is not enough; you must know how you are different. In 1983, psychologist Howard Gardner wrote a book called *Frames of Mind: The Theory of Multiple Intelligences*. He outlined a model with seven dominant forms of intelligence. His chief contention was that we each gravitate to one of these forms. (The seven forms included linguistic, logical, musical, spatial, intrapersonal, interpersonal, and bodily-kinaesthetic. The model has since been updated to include naturalistic.)

Although Gardner's theory has come under scrutiny for its simplistic categorisation, for matters of MEGA motivation, this is a useful framing. There are endless combinations and kinds of intelligence. You just need to understand one: your own. There is a creative domain, or multiple domains, that you are most suited to. Understanding your weirdness depends on deciphering how you are differently intelligent. What is your unique cocktail, your dominant way of processing? How are you wired? How are you weird?

Once you acknowledge that every person on earth is weird and different, this should immediately make you more interested in your fellow humans and invite compassion. How are they thinking about the world? What can you learn from them? What unique struggles are they up against? How is their weird wonderful? This offers a lovely new social disposition.

Creative success follows from understanding your weirdness. A great bit of advice from producer Rick Rubin: "Try for the things you want to see in the world, instead of trying to make things you think other people will want." The first step is to understand what you care about, what you like, what you want to see more of. Making things you think other people want is a sure path to failure. The more you trust your own tastes, the better those tastes will become. If you place the focus on making worthwhile things, then both journey and destination are taken care of.

It should be the easiest thing in the world to be yourself, but we live in a pressure-cooker world that prefers groupthinkers over individuals. We worry what people think, we avoid failure, we cling to labels of ourselves. And we always forget that our greatest creative heroes were utter weirdos. We don't use that term now; now we call them mavericks, trailblazers, pioneers, game-changers. Hunter S. Thompson said, "Weird heroes and mould-breaking champions exist as living proof to those who need it that the tyranny of 'the rat race' is not yet final." Your creative idols could not have achieved what they did if they had followed conventional wisdom. Creative firebrands are obsessive about their craft; they follow strange paths, and they see things other people do not.

Georgia O'Keeffe said: "To create one's own world takes courage." This is especially true when you are faced with motivation that asks you to do things differently. We are so anchored by life paths: best practices, acceptable ideas, social norms, conventional wisdom. But here is an intoxicating proposition: What if we could all start to become ourselves? What if we all start to do things differently—in our own way—and unlock creativity that way? But this approach requires faith in our own creative potential, and it takes courage. The most important trait required to ignite a creative life is courage: the courage to fail, the courage to try, the courage to be different and to pursue things with no immediate payoff, facing the murky path ahead and ploughing on regardless because you like the way the wind feels on your face.

Things get easier the longer you keep at them; but expect to fight feelings of inferiority, pretension, and bewilderment as you start out. In carving out paths that others do not understand, you're exploring unknown territory and taking risks for reasons that will seem foreign to your friends and family.

A quarter of the way through the twenty-first century, at the start of the AI revolution, you might think that your individual contribution through creativity is fast devaluing. I have a different take. There is only one response to the assault of the AI average: be more human. Be the most authentic version of yourself possible. If you find your motivation, your individuality, and make things with that frame of reference, no AI model can replace you. In art, science, business, or life, if you keep working on problems that you care about, other people will also care. Humans will always be more interested in humans than machines. The MEGA approach will still be relevant even in a world with creative AIs (and we are not there yet).

In the swamp of AI slop, your weirdness is the new currency. The more authentic and individual your point of view, the greater your value. AI will undoubtedly offer fantastic opportunities to expand the limits of what we can do, but I expect we will always rely on human creativity—because the future we want is human-centric.

I'm still figuring out my own motivation. After many years of searching, I still lie awake in the small hours and question everything. I'm slowly learning to be comfortable wearing many hats and bringing creativity to bear in different ways. In my day job, I lead a team of actuaries working on new products. Outside this, I'm a writer researching creativity or health or whatever stokes my curiosity. I'm also a parent, and there are few roles more creatively demanding and rewarding. Now and then I compose songs on the guitar. I love to cook, read widely, surf the Cape Town shore, tend my garden, and travel as much as I can afford. I now invite many streams into my life that require creativity without labelling myself as anything but *weird*. I don't need to master any of these domains. I don't need to make my living from all of them. These pursuits are magnets for creativity and avenues to engage with the world more deeply.

If at any time I seem to suggest prescriptions for creativity, ignore these. Individuals find their own way. The only prescription I recommend is a general one: cultivate your uniqueness with creative action. Your weirdness is your superpower and your creative currency. Listening to your authentic interests and tastes, and leaning into creative engagement, is how you traverse spaces of infinite possibility. To be maximally creative, you must have the courage to be yourself. Be weird!

Creative Domains

On opposite sides of Central Park in New York City, you will find two monuments to human culture. On the East side, rising in pale limestone behind grand columns and sweeping steps, the Metropolitan Museum of Art imposes on the park fringe, housing a long history of magnificent artistic achievement. On the other side, the West side, a statue of Theodore Roosevelt keeps watch over a sublime collection of scientific and technological secrets hard-won over thousands of years of human progress: the American Museum of Natural History.

Two tributes to cultural evolution; two collections of creative progress. They balance each other beautifully. The Natural History Museum celebrates our science; the Met elevates our cumulative craft. Science and the arts, complementary ventures, essential pillars of culture. Both sets of curations capture only a fraction of our achievements, but these buildings embody the broad and different domains of creativity. Both imperious, essential, and built from the collective creativity of our species.

The ideas you choose to work with shape your life. Creativity can start with a problem or an idea. Choosing the right kinds of creative projects brings joy, engagement, and purpose. Ideas are the units of creativity. Problems are what creativity is applied against. Choosing the wrong problems causes frustration and wasted years. Chasing the right idea can change your life. At the final reckoning, you are the sum of the things you have engaged in. Your creative life is your personal history of ideas and problem-solving.

Before we proceed, we need a language to talk about creative work. Brian Aldiss said this: "Whatever creativity is, it is in part a solution to a problem." Creativity is about questions and answers, problems and solutions, and the ideas between them. Ideas are the pieces of the puzzle. We use ideas to solve and express. Some people like to say that ideas swirl around in the sky and we simply pluck them out, but this is too simplistic. Ideas are in endless supply and in endless configurations, but we only find them when we're receptive. Ideas need contexts and domains to adhere to, and the more we immerse ourselves, the more we discover.

In the context of MEGA creativity, we need to recast words like "work" and "problems." These words are weighed down with the expectations of an industrial world. "Work" is creativity applied to problems: exploring ideas relevant to the problem, generating new ideas, and shaping these ideas into the best solution. Problems are the subdomains of creative application. Throughout this book I'll talk about problems, solutions, ideas, projects, and work.

Meta-problem-solving

We pursue better problems so that we can have better ideas; this is why the work of motivation is always ongoing. Humans are concerned with problems of understanding, problems of perception, of expression and beauty, of human nature. Different types of problems distinguish different domains: art, science, morality, politics, industry. In science and business, we speak about solutions. In other contexts, like the arts, we prefer to talk about *expression* rather than problem-solving. But they refer to the same thing: these are all realms of creativity that use ideas to do useful and novel things.

We choose problems and then uncover and discover ideas to solve them. This is the essence of the creative process. Creativity is the way humans evolve culture and improve our personal lives: building things, uncovering knowledge, making art, and changing the world around us.

Motivation begins with choice: selecting a problem or an idea to engage with. To a great extent, you get to choose what kind of creative life you lead. It is always possible to better direct your limited time and attention to find better problems. I like the term *meta-problem-solving,* where you choose the kind of problems and projects you engage with. The work of motivation can be seen as a kind of meta-creativity: "being creative about being creative." Some problems are unavoidable, the so-called real problems like death and taxes, but for the most part you can choose what to work on. This is a radical idea for many; that your problems are changeable. Careers, work, hobbies, partners, values, how you raise your kids, how you set up a home, how you arrange your life—creative decisions all.

Some problems you will explore and later abandon. Other problems will become lifelong companions. Choosing bad problems can lead to much wasted time but also to learning.

The Motivation phase is where you find and formulate the problems you want to work on. Some problems are well formed already, and other problems you will shape and discover in the next phase of exploration. You can only discover the contours of a problem by wrestling with it. Seeking out new problems and grappling with them informs which projects you will pursue. In art, science, business, or any other sphere, seeking out new problems is how you get to know yourself. You can build a queue of problems to come back to.

Problems are plentiful. Life is better when you are maximally creative about choosing and solving problems. Throughout your creative life, as you age and learn and change and try things, you will return to the Motivation phase. One of the most important questions for young researchers, budding entrepreneurs, or aspiring artists is selecting the next piece of work (the next problem). A creatively engaged person is always on the lookout for what is next, consciously or unconsciously. What project comes next? While solving one problem, you should have your eyes on the next, hungry and curious.

All of life is problem-solving—earning a living, raising children, building relationships, seeking meaning. In this way, creativity permeates every facet of our existence. No part of life is untouched. The quotidian problems of living well require no less creativity than the classic problems in creative work: like those in science and business and the arts. All problems are not made equal, and, when you have a choice, you should be judicious in your selection.

Diverse Domains

Let's briefly explore where problems and ideas live: in the domains of creative work. Creative work can be defined in all sorts of ways: art, music, literature, sports, science, business, crafts, religion, politics. You can choose which domains to dabble in, or you can just choose problems that interest you. Domains are conceptual spaces defined by the type of knowledge required to engage, and the type of problem-solving involved. In each domain the underlying rules dictate what transformations are possible. For example, all domains of writing are underpinned by the conventions of language. Then subdomains are further nuanced with expectations of rules and form: poetry has a structure, sonnets have a style, limericks must rhyme. Some domains are very well defined (like mathematics), and others are looser (like visual arts or psychology).

You are never tied to a problem or domain forever. Whether you are in high school or in retirement, you may always explore new problems—it is never too early or too late. Creativity, in full glory, breaks down borders between disciplines. In the arena of the arts, we solve artistic problems: problems of expression and perspective. We tell stories, paint, make music, create beautiful works, invent new worlds. With art we wrestle with meaning and emotion. Because artistic creativity is emotional and visible, we often mistake it as the home of creativity itself, but it is just one flavour of creativity. In other arenas, we use our creativity to solve other classes of problems—like the philosophical or practical. This is the realm of scientists, craftspeople, inventors, businesspeople, engineers, doctors, and the like. Problem-solvers conjecture new explanations of the world, proffer new technologies, invent products that help others. Projects of real-world problem-solving are often relegated in the creative hierarchy for no good reason. Their worth is no less, nor is their creative engagement. Practical problems need creative solutions as much as artistic problems need new ideas: we need divergent theories, outlandish inventions, bold businesses, and world-changing explanations.

The domains of science seem to converge with better explanations, while the domains of the arts diverge with varied creation. Both hinge on discovery. Art and science are just two formulations. There are infinite ways to structure a domain. In chapter 3, "Generation," we will look at how these problem spaces can be configured. The more creative we are, the more difficult it becomes to define a domain.

Creativity researcher Margaret Boden wrote about *transformational creativity*; this is the development of new domains entirely. New rules for a new conceptual space. Picasso did this with cubism; Armstrong did this with jazz. New fields should push up like flowers, seeded by the creeping foliage of ideas across a fertile cultural ground. Art applied to functional problems becomes craft. Science applied to business problems becomes technology. Art, science, business, technology, sports, crafts—these are all playgrounds of creativity.

Regardless of the type of problem—whether artistic or scientific at heart—all problem-solving benefits from diverse approaches. Some problems require technical analysis; others need intuition and soul-searching—most need both.

The psychiatrist Iain McGilchrist rose to prominence with a theory on the two hemispheres of the brain. In his book *The Master and His Emissary,* McGilchrist advocates replacing the pop psychology of left-brain and right-brain personalities with a more nuanced view of "how the brain attends to things." Essentially, we have two modes: the left-brain grapples and manipulates, and the right brain contextualises (with a more intuitive and full-picture approach). The workings of the right brain cannot be neatly and explicitly captured. And because left-brain reasoning is more rational and identifiable, the Western world has favoured left-brained thinking. This has resulted in much ugliness and discord as artistic contributions are neglected for the brute efficiency of metrics, measurement, and rational approaches.

Creativity demands a full-brain approach. Any type of problem-solving requires both detailed and holistic processing. Take music, for example. There exists a popular fallacy that music is the realm of the right brain. But think about what a musician must do: They must master their techniques and theory (left-brain mode) all while keeping the soul of the music alive (right-brain mode). Musicians can play the written notes with clinical precision; in this way, music is a science, and it becomes an art when the music is infused with feeling and improvisation.

In the pure sciences, we see an artistry of elegance in the prose of our scientific explanations, in the brevity and structure of our proofs, in the design of our experiments.

We must not confuse problem domains with problem-solving approaches. McGilchrist's model shows that each creative domain requires both a scientific and artistic approach regardless of whether the domain leans scientific or artistic.

We all have different values, and this informs how we order the hierarchy of creative ideas and domains. Misconceptions about creativity lead us to think some fields are more creative than others. We like to talk about creative and non-creative work, but all work has the capacity to be creative. Some domains have stricter rules, so it requires more work to apply imagination, but this just makes that field more difficult—not less creative. The most important problems of our time will require cross-domain problem-solving, so it is important we broaden the scope of creative work to all important problems.

Scientists explain the current world, like Newton pondering the nature of gravity and time. Artists imagine new worlds, like J. R. R. Tolkien building the mythos of Middle-earth. What art does is different from what science does. You can ask yourself if you are more world-maker or world-explainer, or even world-changer. Businesspeople, engineers, and other craftspeople change the physical world. The practical problems of craft and service demand both science and artistry. A carpenter can solve a problem quickly by making a functional and comfortable chair. But he can also express himself by making the chair beautiful, with careful selection of wood material, carving ornamental shapes in the handles. We need this blend of artistic and scientific proficiency.

If it helps, you can demarcate the world of creative work into formal components. But it is better not to fixate on classifications and rather stumble into domains by chasing the kinds of problems that energise you.

Domains are loose collections of ideas, maps for your exploration. I dislike the modern tendency of picking domains and becoming pigeonholed. In fact, I spent much of my childhood rebelling against labels. My attraction to creativity research is exactly because of the sprawling hard-to-categorise range of creativity and its impact across societies and people. Most domains offer endless possibility to learn and engage the world. I love seeing a golden thread of creative discovery. My day job as an actuary relies on understanding population health trends to influence and predict behaviour. This is no more or less intriguing to me than working out how to play a new song on the guitar or learning about laminating American Ash to replace my kitchen counters. It's all problem-solving. The techniques of a professional surfer are as interesting to me as the strategizing of a start-up founder. Once you see things this way, no domain is off-limits. Our creativity allows us endless reach.

It's unlikely you will choose domains from the top down. It's more likely that you will find problems that interest you and then you find yourself in the associated domain from the bottom up. Say problems of inheritance and genes interest you; you'll find yourself in the domain of biology and genetics. Say you become interested in the bends and soulful sounds of a pentatonic scale; you'll find yourself playing the blues.

Domains can be narrow or wide. Narrow domains, like chess, have a finite number of rules and elements. Wide domains like music have a far larger array of elements, and the rules are constantly expanding. It seems like there are more creative choices when composing a song compared to starting a game of chess—although they pose different challenges.

Creative domains house sets of problems and sets of ideas. We will later formalise sets of ideas into spaces of search and spaces of discovery. While domains can effectively organise learning and exploration, many wonderful discoveries are made when domain borders are treated as pliable. Artist Max Ernst said, "Creativity is that marvellous capacity to grasp mutually distinct realities and draw a spark from their juxtaposition."

The Curiosity Bull's-eye

Our job in this lifetime is not to shape ourselves into some ideal we imagine we ought to be, but to find out who we already are and become it.

Are you a born writer? Were you put on earth to be a painter, a scientist, an apostle of peace? In the end the question can only be answered by action.

Do it or don't do it.

It may help to think of it this way. If you were meant to cure cancer or write a symphony or crack cold fusion and you don't do it, you not only hurt yourself, even destroy yourself. You hurt your children. You hurt me. You hurt the planet.

You shame the angels who watch over you and you spite the Almighty, who created you and only you with your unique gifts, for the sole purpose of nudging the human race one millimetre farther along its path back to God.

Creative work is not a selfish act or a bid for attention on the part of the actor. It's a gift to the world and every being in it. Don't cheat us of your contribution. Give us what you've got.

——Steven Pressfield, *The War of Art*

We've discussed how we are all weird and how domains form from problems and ideas; now we'll look at how you might converge on specific creative work and how to think about your creative calling.

Notice how you feel when you engage with a problem. Are you interested? Are you curious? Are you excited? Ask more questions: Are you suited to solve this problem? Do you feel moved by the prospect of contributing?

You want to find the work that you'd do for free. Among the many kinds of motivation, I single out curiosity as key. Feeling curious about a problem or idea is the best indicator that it is worth further creative exploration. When I feel curious, what comes next never feels like work. Directing curiosity with other powerful motivations (like helping people, making the world better, achieving mastery) often helps you set a course.

Motivation for work is found in the doing. But what should we be doing? Many cite focus as the most important thing for creative achievement, but how should you narrow focus when you have competing creative priorities and when you're unsure what to focus on?

I contend that focus follows motivation. As you wade into a field, you can watch for signs like: Where does your curiosity linger? What natural proclivities do you possess? Which missions excite you? Your attraction should grow stronger as you approach the flame. And then your sights will narrow.

There are three critical factors that can guide your focus: curiosity, talent, and mission. These levels might be seen as concentric targets for your creative work: fun, flow, and fulfilment.

I've termed this the *curiosity bull's-eye*, a concept to help focus your creative energies. Picture a Venn diagram of interest, ability, and purpose:

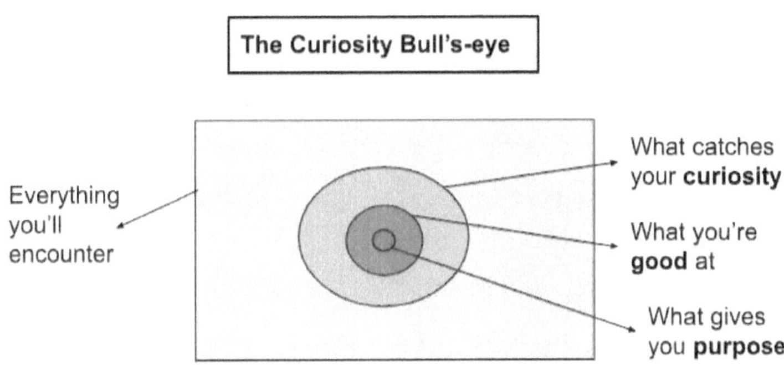

This picture can look very different for different people. You might start with a different factor as the outer layer; for example, start with what you're good at and narrow down. But then you must be wary not to pursue work that you're good at but not curious about. Curiosity is usually the widest net.

Some people have a large bull's-eye; there are many kinds of work that align their interests and talents. Others have small targets because there is a small range of creative work that is fully aligned. Finding this bull's-eye might require throwing many darts, but you should never aim blindly. You should have some hunch about the things you're attracted to.

Some people have always known their bull's-eye. Others must start by throwing darts at the widest circle. The curiosity bull's-eye changes with time, as you change as a person. This is why the work of motivation is never finished. The set of things you're curious about will grow. As your knowledge base and skill set increase, aptitude for new challenges appears. You'll notice how problems and fields are connected, fuelling new feelings of purpose. In his book *Mastery*, author Robert Greene talks about finding your calling as the first important step on the route to mastery. Greene calls this discovering your "life's task": what you are meant to accomplish in your time on Earth. It's a dramatic call to action.

The work of motivation must happen on many levels. You can view creative engagement in levels of commitment: projects or careers, hobbies or missions. Different activities can be viewed according to the elements of the bull's-eye. When I play chess, it's fun, but it doesn't give me purpose—so this is a hobby. I also have projects, like making music, where I'm not particularly talented but I find a great deal of fulfilment in the engagement. These are aspirations. Writing hits all three targets for me: I enjoy doing it, I improve the longer I stick with it, and it bestows a great deal of meaning in my life.

Early experiences are great guides as you look for problems and ideas to engage with. Many mistakenly feel that if they have not cultivated a creative identity by adulthood, it must be because they are not creative. This is fallacy. In most of these cases, creativity was not permitted—by themselves, by teachers, by circumstance.

Your life's task, and the location of your bull's-eye, will reveal itself to you as you pursue your curiosity over a long enough time frame. Whether you believe in callings or not, it's worth investing exorbitant time, energy, and resources to discover the work that changes your relationship with the world. Because it all falls into place when you find work that you feel you're meant to do. When you find work that is aligned with your deeper motivation, you'll start noticing things in higher resolution, with more detail and vivid colours.

Interests

The first layer of the bull's-eye is curiosity. Unravelling your motivation entails understanding what kind of interests and identity to pursue. Motivation is a moving target. As we age, as we learn and create, and as we develop, our interests and ambitions change. Identities are fragile etches in time: they are negotiated, discovered, and constantly evolving. We are not the same people we were a decade ago, or even a day ago.

As you move through the creative phases, you will come to learn things about yourself. By paying attention you can understand your range of interests. Are you a specialist or generalist? The specialist is the hedgehog—one who burrows and digs in deep. The generalist is the fox—one who ranges across fields. The specialist delights in deep focus on one career and field at a time, developing intensive expertise. He has a small creative bull's-eye. It's harder to find, but once he does, he's set, and the creative path is clear. The creative bull's-eye is larger for the generalist. The fox is happy in many fields, but she must be careful about allocating time to projects. Otherwise, she will not become sufficiently engaged or creative in any field because she is spreading her interests and energy too thin.

Are you a fox or a hedgehog? Or are you a different beast at different times? A common proverb says, "A jack of all trades is a master of none, but oftentimes better than a master of one." I don't believe it's better to be one kind of person over another; indeed, there is a wide and fuzzy spectrum of inclinations. Focused people advance single fields aggressively. Rangers put the puzzle together at the ten-thousand-foot view, fetching ideas across disciplines. There are enough problems for us to need both generalists and specialists. Which are you?

To figure out your true interests and your creative callings, it's important to think about what drew your curiosity as a child. When I was younger, at the end of high school, I remember hearing this call and ignoring it. At some level I've always known I wanted to write. I was always drawn to reading and the craft of writing. But because I was good at maths and felt pressure to earn well, I pursued a different career path. And while I have few regrets, if I had not started writing on the side, I would have frustrated a deep creative instinct. It makes me think that there are millions of people with a story similar to mine.

Some people are lucky enough to find and hone their creative passions from a young age, and it becomes an effortless part of their story. They have a head start: tailwinds of motivation. Others need to revisit their childhood selves and ask what delighted them and made them playful. Nietzsche said, "The maturity of man—that means, to have acquired the seriousness that one had as a child at play." Motivation stems from our childlike selves, where we experienced effortless curiosity, connection, and wonder.

Talent

Think of creative work as climbing a hill. Hard work is the speed at which you attempt to climb, and your level of talent determines the incline of the hill. With supreme talent, you'll encounter virtually no gradient, but having no talent means you'll hit a wall. If you love doing something enough, you can spend your life bashing against this wall—and that may be exactly what you should do.

Talent may be more fixed than we realise. We have very real proclivities for some things and not for others; and we should listen to our limitations as we choose creative work. Choose things where you have a chance to make a great contribution. Nature is real—if your intention is to achieve, do not work against it.

Hard work is highly correlated with motivation. Creating something good, people claim, is about putting in the work and logging your hours, but I believe this type of analysis misses the causality of motivation. Steve Jobs said, "I've never found in my whole life that you could convince someone who doesn't want to work hard to work hard."

There is a saying in psychology research: "grit is fit." This idea suggests that many people understand perseverance in the wrong order. The great acts of will happen when motivation is aligned to the work. Activating creativity is not about forcing yourself to do things, it's about harnessing your powerful motivation to do great work. There are exceptions, of course, but most only find that reservoir of resolve when they are sufficiently motivated by the work ahead. I can take weeks to do a small task unaligned to my interests, yet I can spend hours every day writing about creativity without a second thought. Malcolm Gladwell's observation that mastery takes ten thousand hours of deliberate practice may be the wrong interpretation. Hard work follows strong motivation rather than the other way around. It's because you have the motivation that you are willing to perform the ten thousand iterations to mastery.

There is a class of people that operate with a sheer force of will. They will plough through life with a tenacity that is ultimately untethered from their creative interests. But imagine what feats they could achieve if these folks were also creatively energised by their work. The extraordinarily strong-willed among us who find creative challenge and the right historical moment are the ones who change the course of society: the Darwins, the Kings, the Roosevelts, the Mandelas, the Oppenheimers.

Life is more effortless when you are also good at doing the thing you love. Some people have a knack for language, the fast-twitch fibres for sport, an eye for colours, or a head for numbers. It need not define or limit your creative ambitions, but being good at something can foster a love of craft through successful engagement and afford you the chance to be great. Being great need not be the goal, but it's nothing to sneeze at.

When you engage with work closer to your curiosity bull's-eye, you will encounter something called *flow*. Flow is a critical concept in motivation. The first theory of flow is credited to psychologist Mihaly Csikszentmihalyi. He and his teams have studied the phenomenon in depth since the 1970s. Flow is found when someone applies their skills to a problem with the right level of challenge. If the challenge is too difficult, the person becomes anxious or demotivated. If it's too easy, the experience becomes boring. A creative life is about developing skills and applying them to problems. You can raise current skill levels and tackle harder problems, or you can learn new things and try entry challenges—both will provide a feeling of flow.

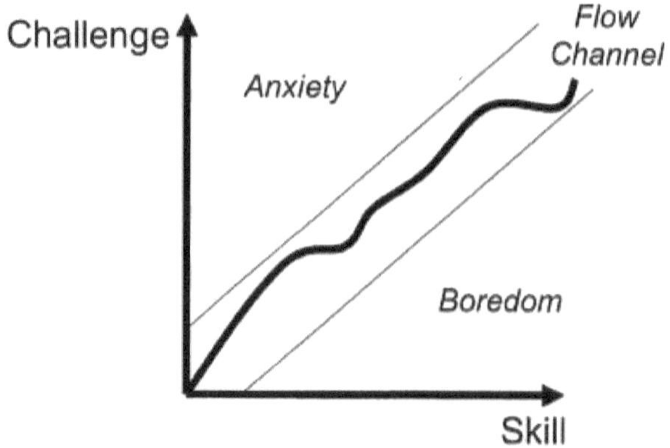

"Flow" concept by Mihaly Csikszentmihalyi.   Drawn by Senia Maymin.

A flow state is close to an out-of-body experience. Flow states will intensify as you choose better problems. According to the research of Csikszentmihalyi and others, flow is marked by at least six factors:

1. Losing sense of time.
2. Losing a sense of self.
3. Feeling intensely focused.
4. Feeling intrinsically motivated to engage.
5. Feeling a powerful sense of control.
6. Merging of action and awareness.

Follow flow; these are the markers to pay attention to in any creative phase. Flow can be found in the search for ideas, in the raw act of creation, on the cutting room floor. Each MEGA phase should be accompanied by varying degrees of flow. Flow is automatic focus. If the work does not offer the right level of challenge, aiming to focus or avoid distraction is futile. The goal in modern life is not to become "indistractable" (as many claim); rather it is to find work that makes you immune to distractions. I like this tip: "Pursue the kind of work that makes you forget to check your phone."

For your creative life it is imperative to pay attention to flow. Do not ignore feelings of disinterest, apathy, dislike, or boredom. How you feel when you're working is more important than talent. You'll find the right work by paying attention to how you respond to creative engagements. Writers can sit in a quiet room with their words for hours on end. Filmmakers love the bustle and social energy of a movie set. You need not box yourself in, but knowing what kind of work you like (and are good at) can be a great guide when choosing creative engagements.

Purpose

Fritz Haber was a brilliant German chemist and a staunch nationalist. At the start of the twentieth century, Haber became obsessed with the problem of solid nitrogen. Nitrogen is an essential chemical for human life, a key ingredient in crop growth. At this time, it was a scarce resource. Nations fought wars and sent hulking ships to fetch guano (bird poo rich in nitrogen) that gathered in great heaps on small islands off the coast of South America, and it was running in scarce supply.

But Haber had been working hard at the problem, experimenting with extraction techniques and laboratory processes. He figured out how atmospheric nitrogen could be combined with hydrogen under a special catalyst to make ammonia. With Carl Bosch and the BASF firm, they developed a new process that synthesised fixed nitrogen at industrial scale. The Haber–Bosch process changed the world. An exploding population could now be fed.

There is a twist in this tale. Nitrogen had another key use at the time: it was a key ingredient in explosives. At the time of the first great war, Haber directed newly available nitrogen supply to produce explosives for mass casualties on the battlefield. One of history's great creative breakthroughs was double-edged; Haber had accelerated the means of giving life and taking it away.

Purpose is the inner ring in the curiosity bull's-eye. The work needs to matter to you. Creativity has no inherent moral compass so it's up to you to decide what is worthy work. Passion is the first part of the puzzle; purpose is the last. You do not need to love what you do *every second of the day*, but the project must seem worthwhile for you to stay motivated. A purposeful creative venture instils some sense of mission that your work can impact the world.

The great creative figures had a very clear sense of purpose, which imbued them with focus, intention, and energy.

Purpose is the final layer of your bull's-eye. Creative work is best when curiosity, talent, and purpose are aligned. Because motivation is found in the doing, you can converge to your curiosity bull's-eye. Test if the work satisfies the three *F* criteria: fun, flow, and fulfilment.

All sorts of things can give you purpose. Your chosen career, your hobbies, your family and home life, your adventures, your intellectual exploration. When you apply creativity to the right things, a tension lifts, and your life will feel more effortless.

Many Motives

It was the quarterfinal of the 2010 French Open. Novak Djokovic was up against Jürgen Melzer, the unfancied 22nd-seeded Austrian. Although Djokovic had a difficult past six months, he was still the overwhelming favourite.

He took the first two sets quickly, almost as if he was going through the motions. But in the third set, Melzer rallied. Incredibly, Melzer started coming back into the match. A few big serves, a backhand winner down the line, and the momentum swung. Djokovic could not recover, and Melzer recorded a shocking win against the odds.

For Djokovic, world number three at the time, it was a heartbreaking defeat. He was hurt. He was stunned. It was a humbling moment for a man who rarely lost. After the game, he sat in his locker room close to tears. This time felt different. He decided then and there he wanted out of the game; he was done with tennis. He set up serious discussions with his coaching team. This was it. He would later call this loss the low point of his career.

Over the next few days, his coach, Marian Vajda, let him vent. Vajda knew Djokovic well. After the complaints and the tears and the release, Vajda asked him a simple but pointed question: "Novak, why did you first choose to play tennis?"

His reply was easy: "Because I loved the game, I loved the strategy and the tactics and the battle, I loved hitting a tennis ball."

Coach Vajda asked another question: "And now?"

Novak sat in silence for a bit and then looked at his coach with a smile. The next day he picked up his rackets and returned to the practice court. This was all he needed: a reminder of what tennis meant to him. The following season he won almost every game in a record-breaking three-slam season, taking the mantle of world number one and breaking Federer and Nadal's stranglehold on the top rankings. Over the next decade, he amassed over one hundred million dollars in prize money, heaps of trophies, and became a convincing contender for the title of greatest to play the game. But it was not about the glory; Djokovic focused on the craft of tennis—on what he loved—and the rest fell into place.

As with any puzzles of people or psychology, there are no easy answers when delving into the full range of human motivation. There are layers upon layers. We have passing whims; hardwired biological drives to find shelter and sex and sustenance and status; deep desires for connection; and mysterious calls to creative engagement. We do things because we are sick, because we are well, because others do them, because we are bored. Our motivations are complex and are often hidden from us.

We all act according to some hierarchy of values. These values are intermingled in complex ways. Values of work and values of living. In work, as in life, we reveal our values with our actions: through the problems we choose. The set of values explored in this chapter are mostly to do with work.

I believe motivation is the hardest part of the creative process. What should you be working on? How do you find new reasons every day to be creative? If you're lucky, your motivation is crystal clear and it always has been. Others might find their way to motivation through trials and failures: cycling through projects until they find the work they're meant to do. The way we choose creative work is a problem in and of itself. We must turn creativity inwards, onto its wielder. Creativity applied to motivation brings our preferences to the surface.

Bad Motives

There is a whole host of factors that have very limited relevance to living good lives: excess money, imagined prestige, the expectations of others. We chase these at the expense of creative engagement, not fully knowing what we're sacrificing. Most people take things day by day, unsure what they want out of life. But at some point, we have all dreamed the wrong dreams. Short-term desires warp and waylay, preventing the long-term seeking and engagement that makes for a creatively fulfilled life. We feed our ego instead of our creative potential.

We become stuck when we listen only to bad motives. We are often motivated by wanting more than we need. It's natural that you solve for the primary problems of living, but the pursuit of excess leads one astray. In the longer term, if you continue to chase material wealth over creative engagement, your enjoyment of life degrades. Your values warp, and you find yourself in the creative desert.

The comedic fireball Jim Carrey said it best: "I think everybody should get rich and famous, and do everything they ever dreamed of, so they can see that it's not the answer." Psychologist Tal Ben-Shahar calls this the arrival fallacy: "if I just earn that amount . . . if I just get that promotion . . . if I just get this award . . ." Most cannot comprehend these warnings. It is in our cursed natures that we need to get rich and famous before we realise that it's not what will sustain us. Chasing money or status without meaning is like grasping at smoke instead of feeding a fire. The fire will burn out.

Often we simply make choices on autopilot. We fail to see that there are better kinds of motivation: being of service, connecting with people, making beautiful things, having a purpose, loving what you do. You can align these to "earning a living"—the reverse is not always true.

You must trust that great work and mastery of any domain is rewarded. But these external rewards are all downstream of great creative engagement. Exceptional creative achievement always attracts high fees and public attention; see these as welcome by-products, not goals. There is no issue when you enjoy compliments and remuneration for your work, why not enjoy the fruits of your creative labour? But these should not be the primary motivation for doing the work. The primary motivation should always be the work itself.

Part-Time Creativity

I hate to say it, but there are things more important than creative work. Things like having a roof over your head, putting food on the table, being part of a community, having access to healthcare. It's not romantic to raise practical concerns, but you need to solve for these needs while you crack the puzzle of creative work.

We like to think that creativity is something other people do, in other roles, and that creativity is something outside your day job. But when you view creativity as problem-solving, you see that it's relevant to everything you do. Including your current work. Often you just need to bring more creativity to what you're doing. Although institutional structures can stifle creativity, you can lift the quality of your days by using the MEGA process to solve the problems you regularly face. Try to do things differently. Reframe your role. Come up with new ideas and fresh energy. How you engage with people is a great opportunity for creativity. Every field can engage your creative potential if you can figure out how.

If you have money problems, you must find work—and any work will do at first. If you don't have a sponsor or a wealthy family, it's likely you'll have to grind an income in parallel while you work out your creative goals. If your current work or environment offers no creative potential, or is completely mismatched with your ambitions, you will need to plan a transition. Many are unhappy with their current work and ask when their primary creative interest should become their meal ticket. But creative mastery takes time. This is the artist's dilemma. Before you can earn from what you love to do, you need to explore, develop a style, and become proficient. A payday is certainly in your creative future, but it's not your primary goal, and you must find ways to feed yourself so that you can keep developing your craft.

Sometimes you must be prepared to do other things to fund yourself. I term this *part-time creativity*. Life's not fair—if you don't live in aristocratic times (when the leisure class sponsored art), or if you don't come from a wealthy family, you must be resourceful. Filmmaker Werner Herzog, as a young man saving up for productions, worked night shifts at a steel factory in the grey Munich winter. Even after considerable success as a composer, Philip Glass worked as a New York City cabbie to support himself. Think of Einstein at the patent office, Kafka at the insurance firm, Vonnegut at a car dealership. No creative life runs linearly. You have this option to keep the creative work part-time and turn to other means for money.

Fitting in creative engagement outside your day job raises all sorts of challenges of focus. The depth of your immersion is limited, the time you can give your projects is fragmented, your energy is depleted; but sometimes life demands this compromise. I wrote this book on the side, getting up early before work to write and often researching late into the night. In these twilight hours, I discovered that writing is a passion—something I'd do for free. And as I write thousands upon thousands of words, I improve. No permission required, but you discover that the hours in a day are short.

A benefit of allowing your creative life to have multiple parts is that you can keep trying new things. Even when you're engaged with work that you enjoy, you may experiment with new creative projects. You can employ creativity in your day job and chase it in projects outside. As long as you keep flexing your creative muscles and stay true to your motivations, you'll figure it out.

Coming Alive

Before you worry about labels and work identity, ask what makes you feel alive. Creativity is the antidote to apathy. What interests you, what challenges you, what connects you to others? This is different for every individual. Work divorced from creativity deadens the soul. For most, the primary driver to work is to earn a living—and unfortunately the focus is more on earning than living. We forget what we sacrifice as we play social games of prestige, competition, and money-making. There is a whole different class of motives when you look at work differently. We might slowly replace the remuneration and status motivation with aims such as activated curiosity, aligned interest, feelings of purpose, and coming alive. When you look to work as an opportunity to engage the world creatively, the work becomes the motivation. It's this feeling of *aliveness* that we're all after—without fully knowing it. We radically neglect this most crucial element: how we feel when we're working. Aliveness is loving what you do, looking forward to the day ahead. Although it's become cliché to say, the best motivation is enjoying the process, the journey, the phases of creation.

Author James Carse wrote a book called *Finite and Infinite Games*. He describes finite games as those that are played for the purpose of winning, whereas infinite games are played because you want to continue playing. Infinite games get better the longer you play. You should seek work that feels like play. This is the sign that you have found something aligned to your motivation. You know you are playing an infinite game when the reward for good work is more work. Infinite games are fuelled by an intrinsic motivation and a positive-sum result. You want the types of games that offer limitless creative engagement. As you deepen understanding or hone craft, these infinite games get better, and your connection to the work and vision of possibilities expands. Writers and musicians and painters get better with age. Scientists expand their fields as they compound their knowledge with time. Businesses become empires that change society. Families grow closer with shared experience.

A quote from Mary Oliver to close this chapter: "The most regretful people on earth are those who felt the call to creative work, who felt their own creative power restive and uprising, and gave to it neither power nor time."

CHAPTER 2: EXPLORATION

Attention – Mapmaking – Active Learning – Freedom

The cure for boredom is curiosity. There is no cure for curiosity.

—Dorothy Parker

You can't use an old map to explore a new world.

—Albert Einstein

Exploration is the searching colour of sky blue. This is the phase of learning, of taking in ideas and forming skills; it is where motivation meets material, where curiosity meets challenge, and where you decide if a field suits your talents and temperament.

In chapter 1, "Motivation," we discussed problem selection. The next phase is about idea selection and exploring your domain from many angles: defining the problem, framing the project, savouring ideas, seeking context, setting down the parameters and constraints. Conceiving of the right questions is as creative as finding solutions.

Exploration is about searching and understanding the problem space. Through acts of curiosity, exploration gathers the material that will later be transformed by generative creativity. Before you can connect the dots, you must collect the dots.

Exploring is mapmaking. The Possibility Space is a vast map of the actual and the potential. Exploration is about traversing the actual. Before you pioneer new territory, you must tread charted ground and search through what has already been discovered. This phase, which you will return to constantly, is the quest to master craft. You'll learn how a great writer writes, how a professional musician prepares, how a successful entrepreneur hustles, or how a top scientist researches. Great learning underpins great work. Before you can be interesting, you must be interested. Exploration can be loose or structured, planned or meandering, directed or wandering. If you apply yourself in the Motivation phase, you will arrive at the Exploration phase intensely curious, with your interests aligned to the problems you seek to solve. The best kind of learning is self-directed and *autotelic*, meaning "having an end or purpose in itself."

You must balance curiosity and craft, playfulness with discipline. If you just practise and don't play, you will lose interest because the magic of new discovery is stifled. If it's all play and no practising, your skills will not improve, and you will become disengaged and disheartened by your limited technical abilities.

Meaningful progress in creative work relies on an expanding base of technical proficiency. Exploration involves both learning of new ideas (knowledge) and assimilation of know-how (skills). Masters in a field develop skills and knowledge that can be retrieved almost unconsciously. Creation becomes easy after thorough exploration.

Exploration can be superficial or in-depth; dip a toe or swan dive in. David Lynch said, "Ideas are like fish. If you want to catch little fish, you can stay in the shallow water. But if you want to catch the big fish, you've got to go deeper."

Attention

In 1831, a young student set off on a great adventure on the HMS Beagle. He was a timid lad from the West Midlands, and he greatly surprised his family when he announced his plans. His destination was the coasts of South America, a gruelling voyage across the Atlantic.

Charles Darwin was hopelessly fascinated by life. The teeming frenzy of animals, the slow complex formation of plants, the drastic diversity of organisms. This pioneering love carried him across the world. Although the conditions aboard tried him greatly, he was buoyed by intense excitement with each visit on foreign soil. He collected samples, made sketches, and inked notes and journals. Countless jars filled his cramped quarters. The other sailors grumbled about the wasted cargo space.

Darwin was looking at the same world as everyone else, but he saw what no one else did: the details, the symmetries in fauna and flora, the change across generations of life that begged an explanation. His observations from this fantastic voyage were later formalised into his theory of evolution by natural selection.

Darwin's theory ranks among the greatest in our history as a thinking species. His explanation of evolution by selection is the extraordinary account of mechanism and detail, elegant in its clarity, and well before its time (Crick and Watson would explain DNA nearly a century later).

Darwin's great leap transformed the science of biology. After this watershed revelation, no one could look at life the same way. Thanks to Darwin, we all notice the connections and potential in living things.

It all started with someone following their keen interest. It started with noticing.

Each of us is an observer, an adventurer, and an explorer in life. The creative life requires attention with intention: where you direct curiosity, what you choose to notice, and how you engage your mind. In vast and novel information spaces, we must develop new ways to explore, which means new filters and new modes of attention. Mary Oliver said that attention is the beginning of devotion—and creativity requires this kind of devotion.

On Noticing

It is astounding how your attention shifts when you begin projects that interest you deeply. You notice things you didn't see before. The painter watches with an eye for colour, seeing the light fall in new ways. The musician listens to the world, looking for harmonies and lyrics and rhythms they can work into their next song. The writer is hungry for stories and for the little details that make text come to life: an abandoned bicycle, a family laughing at a restaurant, a man sleeping on a bench. The entrepreneur starts seeing inefficiencies or inconveniences in society that might be solved with better products.

Venture capitalist and essayist Paul Graham says you must find work whose details engage you but bore others. This is a sign you're working on the right problems. It's when you stop noticing things, when you stop caring about the details, that you need to reinvigorate your creative life.

The psychiatrist Iain McGilchrist said, "Attention is the manner in which our consciousness is disposed towards whatever else exists. The choice we make of how we direct our consciousness is the ultimate creative act: it renders the world what it is." How we see the world determines our sense of what is possible. Attention is how you direct your thoughts; it's the way you spend your time and energy. You become your thoughts eventually, in bursts of attention over the span of a life. Attention with creative intent can be better described as *awareness*. Awareness is a sign that your curiosity is activated. Our experiences slowly shape our work, and what's more, they shape who we become.

When you ignite your curiosity, you open your eyes a little wider in wonder. After any foray into the next phase of generation, you'll be on the lookout for new ideas and material. Little interactions can bleed into your creative work. Ideas dance around in your mind long after the music stops. Small seeds are picked up in your day-to-day experiences—by the park, in the home, in the great canvases of light-filled cities and cloud-covered skies.

Material is paramount for the MEGA phase that comes next. Exploration precedes generation.

When you attempt to generate novel or original work, you will rely on what you have paid attention to. As Amy Rosenthal said, "Pay attention to what you pay attention to." You need to steer your creative attention towards the type of material and ideas you care about. Take in the level of quality you wish to emulate. Exploration feeds an unconscious process. Author Ray Bradbury used to say he read Shakespeare before bed to "prime the pump" of his creativity: he let majestic prose soak into his unconscious. Unconscious observation is one of our great creative aids, but you must find a practice of unlocking what you've noticed. Allow your mind and senses to drift. Often, it's only once we've started a creative project that we realise we're in need of richer material.

The creative life is a never-ending quest for new ideas. The ideas, solutions, or expressions in our projects simmer in our subconscious; we can't help it. We often hear of people complaining about bringing work home, but when our creative pursuits are aligned to motivation, there is no demarcation between work and home. Our pondering, exploring minds cannot be turned off. We become what we visualise repeatedly; we gather ideas in themes, like moss gathering on stones. Reality has a surprising amount of detail. It takes incessant creativity to model this detailed world. Art mimics life, they say, but the reverse can also be true.

We are more engaged in the world when we're engaged in our work. When you're in one of the MEGA states, you're in a state of asking questions, noticing and noting, recombining, and bringing back pieces of the world reforged into your stories, songs, businesses, or whatever your project is. The same observation will be very differently repurposed depending on what kind of creative project you're engaged in. Each observation has many sides; you'll notice the angles germane to your needs.

It has long been known that we project the world in our own image. Our interior states and preoccupations influence how we see things. We see everything through a lens of theory, experience, and preferences.

Brain science explains why we feel as if we tap into different states of attention. By scanning brain activity, we know that we alternate between two major brain networks as we attend to the world. These dominant brain states are referred to as the *default mode network* and the *central executive network*.

The central executive network is activated in planning and active decision-making. This is the conscious state we employ when we plan or direct attention to a problem. The other network, the default mode network, is referred to as the *mind-wandering state*. Psychologist Scott Barry Kaufman calls it the "imagination network." This is a state of mind conducive to undirected exploration, to daydreams and loose attention. You can tap into this mode by engaging with routine tasks: doing dishes, going for walks, and so on. This is a state of mental digestion, where ideas collide and you play with information. Switching effectively between imagination and execution is crucial (we unpack the idea of MEGA Switching in part 2).

The Information

In the post-internet world, we operate in great plains of information. Massive rivers of knowledge run through our society, flooding the fields. We must all hunt, forage, swim.

At no point in history have we had more material to inspire us to creativity—and also to overwhelm us; a paradox of abundance. Writers bask in the light of limitless libraries with lines of shelves that stretch into the horizon. The world of music explodes; we have millions of songs in our pockets. Scientists delight in the knowledge that journals fill up faster than anyone can read them. Papers emerge continuously as we add better and better explanations of the world. With the reach of the internet, it is easier than ever before to become an entrepreneur. You are an Amazon order away from a new book, a search away from a new fact or technique, seconds away from uploading content to share with millions. The dark side of the information economy? They say people have become the product. Attention is as much about avoidance as it is focus. Tech giants, newsfeeds, and smart algorithms vie for our eyeballs—and they are mostly succeeding. How you navigate all the information (including dis- and misinformation) will differentiate you as a creative force and shape your generative potential.

Sturgeon's Law says that "ninety percent of everything is crap"—poor quality surrounds us. Without sound guides, you must do significant search work to find the material and ideas worth exploring. At the core, exploration is about idea selection. What you need most in boundless information spaces is navigation and the ability to filter. As you become more familiar with your domain—your Search Space—you develop the ability to curate. You refine your taste, your nose, your compass. Curation is as creative as production. The way you navigate the space of ideas is full of creative choices. The search decisions you make, the bodies of work you prioritise, the content you elevate; these are the primary influences on your later work.

Google became the world's most valuable brand because they excelled at search optimisation. Optimal search unlocks torrents of creative potential. Google saw the information opportunity of a global internet, and they indexed the world's digital knowledge and made it readily available. The task of each individual is to build their own database of ideas and skills that will unleash creativity in their domain of choice. Search is the phase before discovery; thus exploration precedes generation.

How you sort information will determine what you're able to access in the next phase of generation. Finding quality in the abundant quantity is the challenge. And not just any quality ideas will do; they must be relevant to your current interests and explorations in the sub-search-space at hand.

The great works in your field are clear signals in the noise. Start here if you're unsure how to navigate. The ideas that you study now become future constraints: stepping stones for what is to come. Economist Tyler Cowen popularised the term *infovore*. We live in a new age of access. The challenge is not reach; it is filtering, collating, storing, ordering. In creative life, you are what you eat. You must explore like an infovore before you generate work. Infovores are search experts. They explore with rigour, collecting ideas that crystallise into expertise.

Each infovore operates differently. Modern people may learn from the internet—from tools like ChatGPT, Google, or YouTube. Some are classically inclined, seeking formal education with a preference for books and academic literature. Others find masters to learn from, a practical training. Some may combine all these forms of instruction. You must find the methods best suited to your information-gathering needs.

Infovores are voracious readers. A carefully curated book list is one of the secrets to a creative life. Ideas from all sorts of fields collide in your reading time. Reading widely makes for fertile creative soil and is an enjoyable way to add serendipity into your exploration. With modern tools, the infovore's curation must extend to newsfeeds, AI tools, media, and much more. The meta-skills of searching and filtering are key.

Notetaking

In the Exploration phase, in addition to acquiring the skills you need for your chosen work, you are building a database of ideas. Your ability to be original or generative depends on the quality of the database you've created. These ideas will live both in your mind and in your physical stores. Jerry Seinfeld, a giant among comedians, is obsessive about noticing and recording. Wherever he goes, he carries waiter pads with him. The little observations he jokes about in his stand-up—airplane food, men versus women, useless jobs—are material gathered while observing people and making notes.

Writing this book opened my eyes to one of my major creative shortcomings: taking good notes. There are many valid reasons why we don't make good notes. Finding a system is difficult. A phone is soulless compared to handwritten ideas. But then paper is hard to manage. Note-taking also risks taking you out of the moment. The act of capture may prevent further attention. This natural tide of resistance to recording your exploration is all the more reason to work harder at your system. You lose so many good ideas when you don't write them down. We don't like to acknowledge the fallibility of our memory, but we forget things constantly. There are two elements that make something memorable: strong emotional attachment and novelty. Given many of the ideas we want to preserve for later fit neither of these descriptions, it's likely we'll forget things that would aid our generative work.

The best note-takers develop rich stores that they later recombine into creative output.

The creatively prolific among us find myriad ways to connect with the world, and they write their ideas down.

While living in California in his early twenties, the writer and psychiatrist Oliver Sacks took motorbike rides of several hundred kilometres. He would lose himself on these long journeys across open American roads. He held his head close to the bars to increase his speed, and the reverberations of the bike and the changing environs lulled his mind. Sacks was a restless spirit, a wanderer.

He took a notebook wherever he went and spent hours a day documenting his life. His practice of observation was the key to his creative work. Over the course of decades, Sacks kept hundreds of journals. These observations and insights bled into his writing and clinical work, a rich source of ideas and inspiration.

*His book of case studies (*Awakenings, *later made into a motion picture with Robin Williams and Robert De Niro) is based on Sacks's time working at Beth Abraham Hospital. His old patients were brought back to life on the page, because Sacks could recall their ailments, their behaviours, and their interesting personalities. His work was all the more engaging due to the texture and detail of the stories—straight from the notes in his journals.*

Potential ideas are everywhere. In the mundane moments, in the extraordinary adventures, in your slumbers. You must be ready to crystallise these fleeting thoughts, which often disappear before you can grab hold, like mist flowing from the valley. Good ideas often return to you—but some do not. Record things in the heat of their discovery with as much nuance as you can manage; you will be surprised at how much you forget.

Mapmaking

Exploration starts with wanting to know. How was this built? What does this mean? Before you find the frontier, you must search the current lands. Giants have flattened the ground around us; why not stand on their shoulders for a better view?

The best kind of exploration takes you right up to the borders of what is known. In the Motivation phase, you chose a domain of problems and ideas. The Exploration phase is about searching this domain to see what has already been discovered. You may have to go deep into the territory to fully comprehend the scope and nuance of the problems. You may have to travel far before you fall in love with the land.

The exploratory phase of creativity requires mapmaking: searching, documenting, scouting, reconciling, cross-checking, wandering. You are making models of the world. This is the part of the creative process that entails building knowledge maps and filling skill gaps. To start, you absorb the ideas of others. Then you start on new frontiers, new angles, uncharted territories. It is at this point when you see the scope for generative work. Amateurs see maps in low resolution; masters see maps in technicoloured detail. Fully creative minds can see the actual and the potential. The more you spend time in a worthy creative domain, the more dimensions you notice, the better the view.

Search Space

Much of your domain has already been established. The *Search Space* is the set of ideas that have already been discovered (and recorded). Then there are ideas still undiscovered, the *Discovery Space* (more on this in chapter 3, "Generation"). Together the Search and Discovery Spaces make up all possible configurations in a particular domain (all the songs possible to compose, all the stories possible to tell, all the explanations of the universe). Exploration is focused on what has already been discovered. Current ideas frame your understanding of the domain and become the fuel to fire generative creativity as the next phase of creative work.

Exploration requires you to find, ingest, curate, and absorb these new ideas. As illustrated, the blue dots in the figure below represent the ideas already discovered. You collect as many of these dots as possible. These are skills and knowledge necessary for this creative domain. The image is simplified because you will find an infinite variety of dot sizes and dot shapes to explore. You collect these ideas, and they reside in your mind, colliding with each other. The more dots you collect, the more you can connect in the next phase in combinatorial possibility.

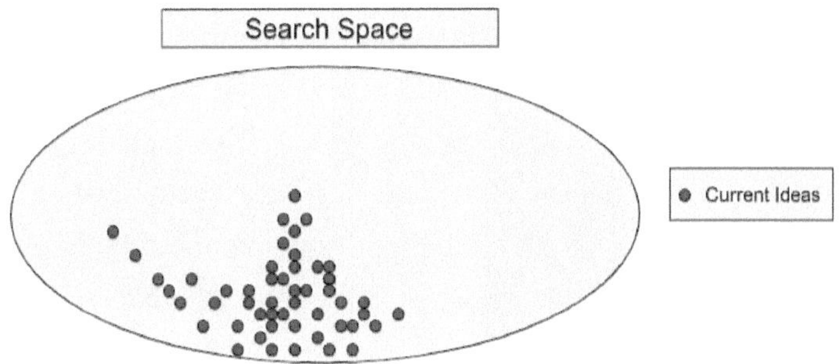

The most exhilarating part of exploration is finding gaps in the map of possibility. Possibilities lie waiting beyond the blue dots of the Search Space: new inventions, original theories, new art, hit songs. Exploration collects current ideas as stepping stones for later generation. As soon as you leave the Search Space, you enter the next phase of creativity: generation. At some point you must jump into the unknown and begin generating. Do this too soon and your skill level and knowledge base will not be sufficient. Too late and you risk paralysing yourself with too many ideas and rules about your domain.

The vast possibilities untouched at the borders of Search Space should instil in you a sense of adventure. Your hero's journey starts by traversing known lands. Before you can find new territory, you must make your way through the already mapped and marked. Great walls of expertise loom large over new entrants to every field. But there are no gatekeepers. Anyone may enter if they are curious and courageous. In these fields are gardens and vistas and beautiful discoveries. In these grounds lie the material you require to actualise your creative potential.

Dot Collection

Exploratory learning thrives in a state of questioning curiosity. Each question leads you to the next idea. One idea after the next, stepping to a bit of knowledge or a new skill: this is how you gather the material required to solve problems.

Listen to your own questions. They further reveal your interest and curiosity. Answering questions rapidly will propel you through a unique path in the Search Space. Curiosity-led exploration is the fastest way to the frontier of your domain. You are developing the ability to reframe a set of problems. Exploration is not only about finding ideas but also about hanging these ideas together in a coherent way. You should have multiple models of the world. A problem can be seen from many vantage points. This exploration and these questions develop the frames you will use to generate new ideas.

Creativity is stereotypically thought of as dot connection. Exploration is the crucial step before that—this is dot collection. As you map your creative terrain, you collect dots. Ideas are dots, experiences are dots, failures and successes are dots, different perspectives are dots, new skills and techniques are dots.

You require these dots before you can be generative. The method of dot collection varies for everyone. The generalist opts for variety; specialists look for dots of a certain type. More dots, more ideas—and more interesting combinatorial possibilities.

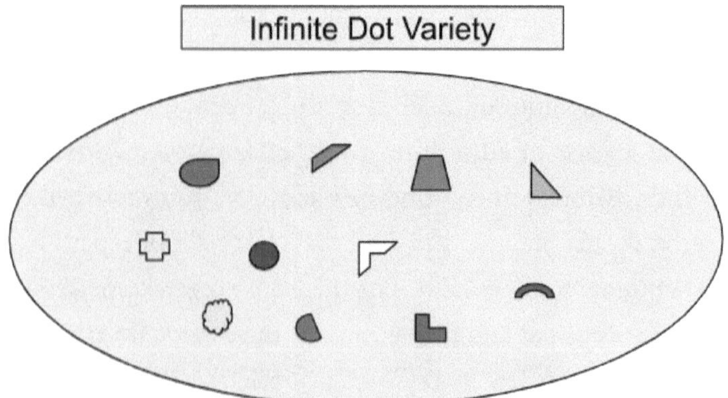

The best companies in the world pay for their talent to explore. Conferences, travel, new courses—these are all opportunities to collect new dots to bring back and improve their products and services. How do you find new ideas in your work? How can you change the culture of your workplace to be more inquisitive and innovative?

While making *Ratatouille*, the animated film about a rat training to be a chef in Paris, Pixar studios sent their animators and producers to the French capital. They observed Michelin chefs in their restaurants, and they looked at the little details: how staff interacted, how food was prepared and delivered, how the kitchen operated. They went into the Parisian sewer system, looking at how the pipes and drain systems were connected, at the materials used, at how deep the sewer sunk down into the bowels of the city. How would a rat navigate this subterranean world? The team brought back the detail that would later bring their film to glorious life. The audience can always tell when you have done requisite exploration. Details are essential. You must study the map. No dot is alike. Subtle differences in an idea can set you off on new creative trails. The more colours and shapes and sizes you collect, the more interesting combinations in the Generation phase.

I'm an amateur guitarist who loves learning new songs. The more I explore a particular piece of music, the more new dimensions reveal themselves. It astounds me how many ways there are to play the same song. The other day I learned the great and ubiquitous "Don't Know Why," made famous by Norah Jones. I copied the original note for note, and at first it sounded great, but after a while the song felt stale. I then took my own advice and carried on exploring. I went and studied how Pat Metheny, the virtuoso jazz guitarist, covered the song. It blew my mind. The soul of the song was still there, but with gut-punching new chords, an original introduction, and luxurious riffs. I copied this version also. My exploration could have stopped there, but then I found the version of the song recorded by a cappella group Take 6. Again, it was completely different with wonderful harmony choices and sustained melody lines. It was only with deeper exploration that I could see the vast range of choices one can make. And I collected more dots.

Much of the creative process cannot be planned because it must unfold naturally. Our creative journeys require open-endedness, moving in whichever direction feels right. There are many ways to cover the terrain. Sometimes distractions are not distractions but rather opportunities to wander. In every state, distractions can be seen as off-ramps to explore new ideas. In the Exploration phase, you must mix wandering and studying as you explore your field, incorporating both structured and unstructured learning.

It is through wandering that you find interesting new angles and ideas: new dots. Cross-domain discovery happens when you range. Centuries ago, we had domains and specialties that were not as well-defined or developed, so capable thinkers engaged in remarkably diverse exploration. Astronomer and mathematician Johannes Kepler's *Harmonice Mundi* (*The Harmony of the World*) applied musical ratios to planetary orbits. In his master's thesis, famed computer scientist Claude Shannon showed that Boolean algebra (a form of symbolic logic) could be used to design and simplify electrical circuits. Technologist Steve Jobs took a college calligraphy class and later applied that aesthetic to the Macintosh's typography and interface design.

Domains exist to help us classify types of creativity, but there are no real borders between ideas. Small-world thinking restricts your creative range and progress. Of course, you must prioritise the ideas and skills most relevant to the problem and interest at hand—but exploration requires looking beyond artificial borders.

Active Learning

I love food. In my life, food is my favourite example of exploration. I love how feasts bring people together. I love the way a good meal can make your day. I love the sharpness of garlic with avocado, the smell of fresh bread on a slow morning, and the way a good cut of meat transforms into something wonderful under a slow roast. I love the endless combinations of flavours and textures and temperatures.

I grew up in a family that appreciates good food (and coffee). You can travel the world in your kitchen—pasta in Italy, stir-fry in Thailand, quesadillas in Mexico, butter chicken in India, braai meats in South Africa. Cooking is a rich and essential creative domain with a layered cultural history.

There is a passive way to explore and enjoy food, and then there is the more active avenue. For most of life, I've enjoyed food through consumption—I've simply loved eating. While I am still firmly in the Exploration phase, my learning has become active—I cook! I've focused my efforts on a few classic styles and dishes, and wonderful things are happening in the kitchen. My cooking journey is a case study in exploration. To inform my learning, I use YouTube cooking videos, recipe books, and generally follow my nose after sampling something good. The internet is an endless store of tips and techniques. With active exploration, the fundamental principles of cooking emerge. You learn by cooking (and eating!). Quality ingredients are essential. Your inputs must be fresh. Your kitchen needs a few basic tools—a sharp knife being the most important. Most dishes use a few key star players to build up flavour: salt, pepper, garlic and herbs, and butter (lots and lots of butter). Like all worthy exploration, cooking takes time and is fraught with struggle. I've spent hours by the stove only to have my chicken taste like rubber. Every time I make a new dish, I worry it will be a disaster. But I push on and keep trying. Each new dish attempted adds another dimension to my creative potential to make great food.

Open Curiosity

There is a concept in Zen Buddhism called *shoshin* or "the beginner's mind." It refers to *an attitude of openness, eagerness, and lack of preconceptions.* It might sound a touch naive, but I think we can learn a great deal from children—from beginners. Look at their eager and open approach to new things. They puzzle at the world. They interrogate. They play.

At some points in our lives, the pressures of life whittle down our appetite for exploration. We start to do the things that everyone else expects from us, and we forget our shoshin. Our childish curiosity is not something frivolous—it is the runway light for our creative lives.

The paradox of learning (and life) is that as you grow in knowledge and expertise, you close yourself off to new ideas and approaches. The creative life requires new problems, and the creative approach demands openness to thrive. Closing yourself off leads to a creative death. The shoshin philosophy reminds you that it's about the joy of the work—not the accolades or the payoff. This approach will stave off the closed-mindedness that atrophies many creative ventures. It also helps you to avoid hubris and insecurity.

Exploration is more than idle wandering; you want to harness that curiosity as fuel for mastery. More than idea collection, you want to learn how to operate effectively in this field. Learning aligned to curiosity gives you the effortless motivation required to transition from amateur to professional, novice to expert. You can be daunted by the immensity of material available, or you can be amazed and opt rather for a state of wonder and openness. Scott Young, in his book *Get Better at Anything*, said, "Unlike hunger or thirst, curiosity is stoked not sated when we learn more."

The range of your curiosity depends on what kind of person you are. We previously introduced the specialist–generalist spectrum. Someone like Leonardo da Vinci was a generalist, a ranger of the highest order. He started projects with reckless abandon, amassing ideas from disparate domains and connecting them. Contrast Da Vinci with Madame Marie Curie. Curie was one of history's great specialist scientists. Her style was that of a dogged burrower. In her groundbreaking research in radiotherapy, she kept narrowing down the problem. The work called for painstaking detail, isolating isotopes, measuring microscopic activity. With this careful specialisation, Curie discovered new chemical elements such as radium and changed our understanding of radiation and medical imaging, which saved countless lives. Your learning can follow your curiosity, whether that is wide or deep.

Passive and Active

The great music producer Quincy Jones thinks of learning as "left-brain work"—developing technical ability that will expand your creative options in later phases. To be a top musician, he says, you must be able to sight-read and play your scales. There are certain prerequisites for mastery in a field.

There are two forms of learning, broadly speaking: passive and active learning. Passive learning is the kind of exploration where you take in information. You rely on good informational inputs. The quality of input matters a great deal. If you consume quality ideas, your attempts at generation later will reflect this. You are limited by the range and depth of your learning, by the quality of your explorations.

Amateur exploration stops here, with passive learning. There is nothing wrong with this; sometimes this is all you want from an interest. But if you want to activate creativity further, you'll need to take a step forward in your exploration. You'll need to engage in active learning.

Active learning is learning by doing. You can't learn to write just by reading. Active learning, much of the time, looks like copy work. You mirror the creativity you see. Instead of reading, watching, and listening, you learn by writing, making, and playing. Humans share the evolutionary ancestry of chimps, after all, and the older parts of our brains are apelike. We are incredible social learners. Evolutionary theorist Joseph Henrich cites our inherent capacity for social and cultural learning as the secret to our success. Imitation is the secret sauce of our learning process. Copying and learning from others enlists all sorts of ancient brain networks.

When you are curious and driven to learn, you will switch between passive and active learning instinctively. In the same way, you will transition between active learning and the next phase of generation. Active learning is an exercise of simulated generation.

In this phase of copy work and intentional practising, you may feel the pull to try things: this is generative creativity calling. You need not wait for proficiency before you test out new ideas. Exploration and generation can run parallel. The ideas you are ingesting want to be recombined, unleashed in your own style, and your brain cannot help starting to do this. Jump to generation as soon as you feel the impulse. You can return to exploration soon after. You are rehearsing how to get ideas down in your chosen domain. As soon as original ideas come in, you will find yourself thinking about novel configurations, and you're in generation mode.

Masterful creativity requires building a sound technical base in your chosen field—domain-specific learning. While painting, if you want to capture light and shade, careful expressions, and the finer detail, you need technical expertise. This means countless hours at the canvas; improving your technique, taking instruction, studying the masters.

Deliberate practice requires repetition and rehearsal. If your motivation is aligned, the road to mastery is enjoyable. The writing exercises, the scales, the drills you must do in your domain—you do them with pleasure. They expand your creative potential. You want a skill set and knowledge base that is so embedded that you can recall it unconsciously; this engrained exploration is known as *muscle memory*.

Exploration is preparation. If you do the hard work of exploration, your generative flow will not be interrupted by technical inadequacies and shortcomings. You become the vehicle for original ideas more effortlessly. I'd also argue you can more easily notice elements to play with.

Go and watch a video of your favourite musician. Choose someone who is at the top of their game. I'll use the example of Lang Lang, a Chinese pianist regarded as one of the world's best. Watch any of his performances. Notice the ease of play. He is not thinking about the notes but rather how to emphasise and space them. There is endless room for expression and interpretation. When the right amount of learning has been put in, creativity is transferred to improvisation: novel interpretation and original stylistic flourishes.

Expertise

Expertise is the result of many years of immersion and active practising; it does not come cheaply. In modern times, everyone's an "expert" demanding equal consideration of their point of view. But expertise is not evenly distributed. Expertise is hard-won through exploration. Knowledge is built from dedicated processing: it takes time and care. If you need to distinguish professional from amateur, look at their basics—experts know the details.

We learn best from other people. In Da Vinci's time, it was common for learners to become apprentices to learn the trade. They would spend time with a skilled master and work intensively on each part of the process. Working with the right person can supercharge learning and speed up your development drastically. You don't know what you don't know—and a mentor can transform your map of the domain.

In certain trade fields like carpentry, you will still find apprenticeship as a formal convention. In the corporate world, you may find a manager or colleague that becomes a mentor. In academia, you'll be required to select a thesis supervisor. The apprenticeship model is powerful, but we have forgotten its importance somewhat in our dislocated times.

Da Vinci was an apprentice to Andrea del Verrocchio, a renowned painter and sculptor. This human-to-human transfer of expertise is sacred. Apprenticeships are a dying tradition that you should seek to revive. Find a hero in your domain and ask them questions. People are surprisingly easy to reach nowadays, and if you show a genuine love of their craft, they're very likely to answer.

Those who can identify quality inputs (ideas and materials) distinguish themselves. A skilled woodworker knows how certain timbers bend. They know when a hard wood is needed and when a soft wood will do. They know when a plank is warped or rotten. A good chef can tell if their ingredients are fresh with a squeeze and a sniff: fresh fish smells of the ocean, quality vegetables are firm in the hand. Good musicians hear immediately when an instrument is out of tune. Top scientists can tell a good experiment from a bad one. Enterprising business thinkers can immediately see if an applicant has the resourcefulness to succeed. There is certain contextual information available only to those with extensive experience.

In Japan, the master swordsmith Yoshindo Yoshihara carries on a tradition over a thousand years old. When forging a katana, he describes "listening" to the steel. He can tell, by the colour of the glowing metal and the sound it makes under his hammer, exactly when to fold, when to cool, when to let it rest.

What seems like mystical intuition is deep attunement—generations of exploration and experiment. In one interview, he described how he could sense flaws in a blade before they appear, saying the steel tells you what it wants. If you try to force it, it breaks.

To most, a raw hunk of Tamahagane iron looks unremarkable. To Yoshihara, it's a living thing, full of potential.

Freedom

My parents were high-school sweethearts. They both went to De Kuilen High School, a government school in Kuilsriver (a large suburb on the outskirts of Cape Town, South Africa). At this time, in the 1970s, the country was at the peak of repression in the Apartheid regime. The ruling ideology embraced extreme conservatism and bigotry. This was not a place to be black, gay, or creative. School and society were set up to produce a very specific type of person: Christian, straight, sport-loving, family-oriented, and regrettably racist.

The story of Nataniël stands out. He was an eccentric boy in the school year between my mom and dad. Soft-spoken and slightly effeminate, they remember him mostly from the odd musical concert. Because of the way school pressures denigrated non-sport or non-academic interests, Nataniël was not remembered as particularly talented, he was just considered weird.

It was after school that Nataniël's story bloomed, becoming an against-the-odds miracle of creative liberation. It turned out Nataniël was a creative force. My parents watched his rise with relish. He succeeded at everything he touched. One hit music album after the next, a blockbuster cooking TV show, a master of stage and screen. Music, cooking, writing, comedy—Nataniël did it all. From school weirdo to national treasure. His nickname, "Kaalkop," will always be associated with local creativity: an irrepressible talent in the most repressive of times. We love the story of Nataniël, but he was an extraordinary case. How many students at De Kuilen did not manage to break their creative shackles?

This last section in chapter 2, "Exploration," explores the freedom required for individual creativity to flourish and range. Albert Einstein said, "To be free means to be independent, not to be influenced by what others think and say." Freedom feeds into every phase of creativity. It is an essential precondition for creativity to flourish. When free speech and thought are limited, creativity is curtailed. Throughout your creative life you need to watch for forces that restrict your freedom. What ideas feel out of bounds? Where do social pressures constrict you? Are you free to explore your curiosity? How you apply creativity is a test of freedom.

The discussion of freedom is different to that of constraints. A musician is happy to be constrained to one instrument as they learn, or to a particular genre. Those constraints serve to focus creativity more potently on problems to make progress, avoiding the crippling effect of too many options. These are voluntary constraints, and internally imposed. These types of constraints do not limit freedom; they achieve the opposite: narrowing down creative choice so that we can act.

The anti-freedom forces described in this section are anti-creative, and they involve limiting beliefs. Anti-creative forces stop creativity happening; they prevent individuals from solving their own problems and exploring the creative work suited to them. Repression and restraints take the form of *de rigueur*, stunted ideology, coercive programs, rigid educational systems, or tyrannical regimes.

The importance of freedom runs deeper than nice-to-have notions of creative choice. Personal and ideological freedoms determine the extent to which individuals may liberate their potential. Fascist, authoritarian, and variants of collectivist society models do not allow individuals to fully self-actualise. Anti-freedom forces were on full display when millions of Soviet farmers starved to death because they were not allowed to farm for their own families. Unfortunately, restrictive thinking has a way of spreading. Top-down agendas, however well intended, will always stifle creativity. For creativity to flourish, free-thinking persons must be able to act unfettered.

Free Society

There are different types of freedom. An individual can be restrained even in Western liberal democracy if they operate with bad ideas that limit agency. Our companies, families, and organisations impart ideologies and values that influence creative choice. Often we are unaware of the water in which we swim. Social judgement stifles courage and originality in powerful ways. We check ourselves, adjust our opinions to fit the crowd, and scale back our ambitions.

In the mid-nineteenth century, John Stuart Mill, the British philosopher, published a defining treatise on the nature of freedom and the forces that society imposes on individuals. Why is this relevant? Because individuals are the vehicles of creative action. Time and again we see regimes fall and civilisations crumble when they stifle the individual.

In his lasting work *On Liberty*, Mill said, "As it is useful that while mankind is imperfect there should be different opinions, so is it that there should be different experiments of living . . ." Individuals who cultivate their identity and live unconventional lives undergo these "experiments of living." These experiments are what drives individual and societal development. A free person must have the ability and appetite to experiment. In the formulation of Mill, acts of curiosity and creativity are crucially important to maintain dynamic and creative societies.

Mill goes on to say that "in suppressing an idea, a society runs the risk that it is suppressing the truth." Conformity threatens the diversity of these experiments, and thus the chance of discovery and progress. In the MEGA framework, curiosity and creativity (and their constituent phases) provide the thrust, the ideas, and the tools for these experiments of living.

For creativity to thrive widely, ideas must be allowed to be spread freely. The spread of ideas allows nuance in our collective thinking. Bad ideas must see the eradicating light of day. Evil ideas must meet their end in public for all to see. Good ideas should be afforded the chance to spread. Individuals must be allowed to adopt and discard positions. If we don't allow redemption, we don't allow improvement. We must allow room for error and then laud error correction. We can still have punitive consequences for bad actions, but for revocable errors we must allow error correction. Freedom of ideas and speech is upstream of flourishing creativity.

Our creative decisions carry moral weight. While it might be necessary to regulate some outcomes, the creative process must be allowed to run untethered by the ever-reaching arms of politics. It must remain each creative individual's decision what to engage in. Only impact on others should be judged.

You need not look far for places and times where creative expression was forbidden. Certain systems of thought and governance shackle the individual. Orwellian conformity roots out creativity before it can take flame, and sparks are trampled out by the large feet of the state. The unappreciated truth is that creative expression and novel problem-solving are fragile endeavours. If we are always monitored, and if our unconscious cravings to conform are too strong, we self-censor and direct our attention away from the creative avenues that bring beauty and truth and progress. We die a million creative deaths.

Free Range

We have a creativity problem in formal education. Famed educator, the late Sir Ken Robinson said, "My contention is that creativity now is as important in education as literacy, and we should treat it with the same status." Our models focus on content over approach, what to think instead of how. We do not cater to individual creativity at schools.

Ask a class of preschoolers, "Who is creative?" All the hands in the class shoot up. Ask the primary schoolers, and half the hands go up. By late high school, almost no hands go up. It seems we systematically stamp out creativity in schools. A mix of peer pressure and increasingly irrelevant school syllabi has caused this. We pick problems for kids instead of letting them pick their own. This causes a motivation issue, a degradation of self-direction that leashes exploration. After the set work is done, little time is left in the day for exploration.

Schools try their best. They teach kids the facts of the world and attempt to impart skills. But this type of learning is narrow. Traditional schooling fails most children in some way. Most often, they cannot cater to individuals, and fail to show children that there are unique paths that they might follow. Young minds are subtly dissuaded from following their primary interests—and they're prevented from key forms of self-actualisation. Teachers can't adapt to the many and messy minds they encounter. Each child is different, and schools simply don't have the resources for individual programs.

Many parents cede the responsibility of education to schools when they are sorely needed in the cultivation of their children's creativity—as role models, as guides, as liberators when schools overreach and overteach. This is especially true when a child's creative talents and proclivities deviate from the standard school curriculum: like the future film directors with fierce visual intelligence, the future entrepreneurs with incisive social intelligence, the future scientists with singular research focus. They flail in maths and English class or some part of the "core subjects," getting grades that slowly break down their spirit and confidence. Between parents and schools, we need new ways to engage diverse creative needs.

Many schools teach children that the world is small and that most things are already figured out. Institutions want young people to pick identities and then pick careers. Then we can put them in industries and plan our economies. In this way we make the world codifiable. But by doing this we reduce people to workers and make the world less interesting for everyone.

We should be showing them the frontiers. What is currently known is an infinitesimal fraction of what we might know and create. We should be showing kids the power of their creativity—a boundless potential—if they learn to harness it with discipline, in controlled settings.

In the right doses, we must show each other the massive potential for discovery in every domain. Our known unknowns are vast, but our unknown unknowns could be endless. There is a level of certainty that we provide for children that is necessary in an anxious world, but we go too far when we hem in their dreams and their creative potential. Like Truman Burbank in *The Truman Show,* we keep individuals in the tepid towns of our past creation, living in endless loops and fixed horizons. Before precious creative energy is wasted or misdirected, they must be shown that endless Search Spaces are waiting. We must teach them how to set sail.

The big problem today is that we don't know how to teach creativity at scale. Many of our schools and organisations fear free exploration instead of fostering it. Of course, we can help provide knowledge and instruction—but harm is done when exploratory spirit is stifled. Creativity is killed before the blooming generation can occur.

Having creative freedom empowers the choice to go wherever your curiosity takes you. This often means interdisciplinary exploration. Some of the greatest creative breakthroughs came from fetching ideas in unexpected places. Some of the best ideas for your field likely lie outside of it. This creative freedom results in the rebellious and revolutionary ideas that progress things:

in science, art, technology, or the other. It is open-ended exploration that leads to great discoveries. Alexander Fleming discovered penicillin in the mould of a forgotten petri dish. You may find good reasons to discontinue explorations—moral reasons, convention, fear—but if you feel undue and illiberal influence when you explore, this is a sign that your freedom is restricted.

CHAPTER 3:
GENERATION

Just Start – The Open Mode – Tinkering – Infinite Spaces

In every age there come forth things that are new and have no foretelling for they do not proceed from the past.

—J. R. R. Tolkien, *The Silmarillion*

The principal mark of genius is not perfection but originality, the opening of new frontiers.

—Arthur Koestler

Generation is the hot red colour of a forging fire. Finally, we are here. The Generation phase is what most people talk about when they talk about creativity. This phase is about creating things anew—novel output, new insights, and original works. It's the phase that looks most like magic. If exploration was about search, generation is about discovery. If previously we spoke about dot collection, this is the phase of dot connection.

Generation harnesses our innate and incredible facility for recombining old ideas to arrive at the new. This is the phase for divergence, for out-the-box views, for tinkering. The Generation phase is your boundless sandbox, where you break new ground, fusing the intuitive with the rational.

A great tragedy today is that most people do not feel that they have ability or licence to generate. They are not creative, they say, so they never venture past exploration. Getting more people to be generative, illuminating your inherent creative capacity, is perhaps the most important theme of this book.

The previous two phases were largely about igniting and following curiosity. The next two phases (Generation and Amelioration) are about creative production. We can talk about two phases that forge output: hot creativity and cold. Generation is hot creativity—this is the imagination phase—bringing new ideas into the world. It's this kind of creativity that Sir Ken Robinson referred to as *applied imagination*. Cold creativity is amelioration: curating, shaping, and forming these ideas and solutions into finished works.

First up in this chapter, we'll discuss why you should start to practise the work of generation as soon as possible. We'll outline something John Cleese calls the *open mode*. We'll then marvel at the power of experiment and the necessity of open-ended discovery. Last, we'll look at models of Possibility Space—how every creative domain is a space for infinite reconfiguration.

Just Start

In January 1961, Robert Zimmerman left his sleepy Minnesotan hometown and took a bus to New York City. He had only ten dollars in his pocket and a hunch that Hibbing was not the place to make great music—and that New York was. He wanted to live and breathe music, as much of it as he could find and wherever he could find it. He was nineteen, hungry, and unknown. It was freezing cold—he later said he pretended to be a college student just to sneak into the YMCA for a cheap place to sleep.

His destination was the West Village, where, in the basement bars, juke joints, and rowdy restaurants, people were composing and performing the kind of music he loved. Greenwich was where the music was happening and where the folk scene was thriving.

He had a loose plan to seek out Dave Van Ronk, who played the Green Room, and was known as the Mayor of MacDougal Street. He was kind to young artists. Zimmerman soon found the Mayor and did the only thing he knew how to—he played for him. Van Ronk liked what he heard. He introduced Zimmerman to other musicians and new kinds of music, helping him deepen his understanding of American roots. Zimmerman soon became part of the scene.

Robert Zimmerman is still going sixty years later. Today he is known as Bob Dylan. A Hail Mary from Hibbing. This was his start.

For this most important phase, I offer two simple syllables: **just start**. Be Bob. When you have an idea of what you want to do, get going. Get going even if you aren't sure. Picasso said, "To know what you're going to draw, you have to begin drawing."

How you start, and what you start on, is not important. The details get in the way only if you let them. Whatever scratchings or scribbles you have, start there. Whatever you picked up in the Exploration phase, use these as your stepping stones. Your creativity is realised and discovered in the doing. Too many people battle with the idea that they might be generative; they do not believe that they might make a novel contribution to the world. Bad cocktails of limiting beliefs bubble over when it comes to our creative potential. We have this sense that we're not special, and we lack the audacity to be original, so we never start.

What if you just get going and see what happens? Great things can happen if and only if you start. We mentioned courage in the Motivation phase. It may take a long time before you're any good, but that doesn't matter when the work is the reward. In part, this is about lengthening the creative runway of your life. You want to develop the generative habit as early as you can—because the more you develop the generative habit, the better you get.

Lose Yourself

As you attempt to be generative, be wary of the forces that stop you creating. Your greatest challenge will be getting out of your own way. The author Ray Bradbury stuck the following words above his typewriter as he created new worlds: "Feel—don't think." Bradbury claimed that the intellect is a great danger to creativity. The philosopher Wittgenstein said something similar: "Don't think, look!"

Generative creativity is about feeling and intuition and tapping into something we do not understand well. Thinking comes next, in the Amelioration phase. In the Generation phase, you must simply keep imagining.

When you start out in the Generation phase, the aim is to lose yourself. Artist John Cage once described the process of losing himself as follows:

> When you start working, everybody is in your studio – the past, your friends, the art world, and above all, your own ideas. But as you continue painting, they start leaving, one by one, and you are left completely alone. Then, if you are lucky, even you leave.

It takes practice to become generative and to relinquish yourself to flow, and to create and produce without judgement. We spoke about flow in chapter 1, "Motivation." As you become comfortable in a generative state, new ideas will flow more easily. The generative brain is a muscle. Singer Ed Sheeran describes his generative process as a sewage pipe: he needs to flush out all his bad ideas first before the water runs clean. We have all been contaminated for too long in the arena of the collective average. Begin generating with urgency to clear out all the trite ideas, the clichéd versions, and the pedestrian opinions. Then you can get to the good stuff. This is how you find something worth saying. This is how you develop a nose and a body of work to build on.

Your creative mind is always working; coming to the Generation phase is your release, an outlet for your irrepressible creativity. It can become a kind of therapy for you. Creativity unrealised becomes noise in your head: a special kind of anxiety. Release your creative tension with generation, and when you are spent, notice how you feel.

There are different ways of knowing things. Philosophers talk about propositional knowledge; this is the left-brain kind of knowledge, that which can be made explicit. Propositional knowledge is everything we can put into words. Creative work helps us express the non-propositional. So much of our creative potential cannot be clearly articulated. It lies within us, internalised but often not clearly expressible until you lose yourself in creation. The non-propositional houses the intuitive, the gut feelings and unconscious faculties that we all possess. Generative creativity often taps into the non-propositional. It's about feeling and listening, and trusting your creative instincts.

Your past labels don't matter when you feel the pull to create. If you want to be a writer, write. If you want to be a scientist, research and experiment. If you want to make music, compose. You can just do things. Don't wait for credentials or permission. A bad writer is still a writer; a bad musician still gets to play. Lose yourself in the attempt.

The Blank Page

There is tyranny in endless possibilities. The blank page looms; the white space blinds you. Do not be cowed. You must tame infinity by starting—any move will do at first. Surprising things happen once you start. But you must not wait too long to make some marks. If it helps, forget all the rules, and the proper order of things, and start anywhere you can. Copy, scribble, scratch. Perfection is the enemy of the good. Total mastery will never be achieved. The perfect conditions will never come. Before you lose yourself to creative anxiety, and become paralysed by a swelling ocean of options, just try something. Pick up the brush, the pen, the instrument. Throw something on the blank canvas; play the first notes of the song, draft the business plan. By taking the first steps, you are starting a flywheel of action. To beat the curse of the empty page, get something down quickly. The hope is that the joy of creation propels you to further discovery, and soon you'll be in clear air.

Do not underestimate the power of the previous MEGA phases. The more exploratory work you have done, the more material you will have to draw from. Even if you aren't consciously aware of it, you'll have more ideas to play with. There is a paradox in that the more you learn the rules, the more limited you start to feel. So, in the early days, enjoy the freedom. Forget the rules for the moment and come up with novel approaches. Something called the Dunning–Kruger effect says people with low ability overestimate their expertise, while actual experts often underestimate theirs. Enjoy your Dunning–Kruger phase.

Start with what you have. By engaging with your generative abilities, you soon realise that you can make things, change things, and shake the walls of your domain. You never know how close you are to a beautiful story, a breakthrough scientific idea, a transcendent piece of art, a transformative product or service. Later, we'll talk about embracing constraints. Right now, you have a chosen domain, a specific style, a unique point of view—start there! Aim your creativity at whatever you are grappling with, and see what comes out of it.

If the hardest part is starting (be that a session, project, or career), imitation is a great way to break inertia and find some momentum. So, mimic! Copy! Steal! Imitate the masters. You have no intention to pass their work off as your own. You pay them a compliment when you use their work to inspire your own. Start with their ideas, play with them, and tweak them. If you apply enough of your own voice, you develop something new entirely.

It's unnecessary to draw bright lines between phases. The MEGA phases blend and bleed together. Imitation is a concept that could be raised in any of the four phases. We adopt motives, learn by copying, and ingest the tastes of others. Stephen King, one of the most generative writers, said "imitation precedes creation." Imitation is an important part of creativity, in both learning and creating. In the Exploration phase, we imitate to develop our skills. In the Generation phase, we imitate to innovate. The work of others is an easy stepping stone to derive something original. They are the first lights on a path to new configurations. Oliver Sacks spoke of *minor* and *major creativity*. Minor creativity is clearly derivation, small steps away from the original work or idea. Major creativity requires some radical leap, where imaginative generation offers something truly new and valuable. When you are starting out, all that matters is that you are working, and the judgement of output must be suspended.

If you follow the MEGA steps in order, you will arrive in the Generation phase with a head full of ideas and hopefully with some skills to accompany them. If you have a natural inclination to your field, you may be generative very early on. On the other hand, trying to be too generative too early can also be dispiriting, so you may need further instruction in the Exploration phase.

A final idea to consider when you start out: aim your creation at one person. Write for someone in particular; call them your ideal reader. This can be someone who you respect, someone who will give good feedback, or simply someone you care about.

In business, develop your product for an ideal user or customer. In music, this means playing for the delight of a specific audience. In science, think about describing your theory or evolving explanation to a mentor. This brings the work to life.

In any endeavour, pick this target person—idealised or actual—and stop trying to write for everyone. It will also quiet the room of critics as you develop your ideas. James Joyce wrote *Ulysses* with his wife Nora in mind. J. R. R. Tolkien shared his work with C. S. Lewis. Feynman lectured to one student at a time. Carl Sagan spoke to "the child who looks up at the stars and wonders." Beethoven composed for someone he called his "Immortal Beloved." Bob Dylan said he wrote for no one but himself.

The Open Mode

In times of stress and stimulation, Paul McCartney dreamt in song. Lyrics and melody filled his tired slumbers. One night in 1964, as Paul was struggling with the meteoric rise of The Beatles and his new stardom, he heard a new song in half-sleep—with lyrics like: "All my troubles seemed so far away". The next morning he woke up, picked up his guitar, and played what he heard in his dreams. The melody came to him almost fully formed. He played it to his bandmates, and to other family and friends, thinking he was playing an existing song; he wanted someone to tell him which song this was. He was shocked to find that no one could place it. The song was his own, an unconscious product of his creative mind. "Yesterday" would become one of the most popular songs in music history.

There is an easy mistake to make here when trying to explain how Paul composed in his dreams: You can marvel that he dreams in song, you can say that he is a genius and you can move on. Or you can look more closely. Genius is a non-answer. I prefer explanations that are messier: more instructive and more interesting. There is no doubt Paul had innate talent for composition, but it is his consistent songwriting practice that compounded his talents into song-making magic.

McCartney is a case study in cultivated openness. Since his teenage years, Paul wrote songs. Even before he met John and the other lads, Paul would write and sing his own stuff. Because of his ability to receive ideas and write them down, he developed the knack for composition. Then he found John Lennon, a creative equal who would spur him on to be even more generative in a fiery collaborative and competitive partnership.

From a young age, Paul learned how to be open to his generative creativity, and this muscle grew stronger. He nurtured this ability until it became automatic, unconscious, to the point that he could write hit songs in his sleep.

Creativity researchers will tell you about the one trait (above all others) that creative people possess: openness. Great creative figures are open to new ideas, to new experiences, and to new approaches. This openness is learned, unlearned, relearned—it is all-important. Openness requires disarming your guard, suspending preconceptions, withholding judgement, and suppressing the inevitable internal criticism that we all face.

Notable creative figures and artists talk about "channelling"—being a vessel for a creative idea that wants to come out into the world. It's been described as such by David Lynch, Bob Dylan, Richard Feynman, and Maya Angelou, to name just a few. They talk about ideas working through them. This vessel-like view of creativity is similar to other descriptions of intuition, dreams, and altered states. Psychologists call this state "flow," artists talk of the "muse," Carl Jung thought that people tapped into a "collective unconscious," and Einstein—like McCartney—found solutions in dreams. Creativity operates in a deep part of our unconscious brains, and we have to do work—and be open—to retrieve what we come up with. Author George Saunders talks about "the ghost" that emerges when someone sits down to make art or work; as if their creative selves are other entities entirely. Here is David Ogilvy reflecting on how we open to our unconscious:

> Big ideas come from the unconscious. This is true in art, in science, and in advertising. But your unconscious has to be well informed, or your idea will be irrelevant. Stuff your conscious mind with information, then unhook your rational thought process. You can help this process by going for a long walk, or taking a hot bath, or drinking half a pint of claret. Suddenly, if the telephone line from your unconscious is open, a big idea wells up within.

These metaphors are imaginative ways to describe tapping into your generative brain. Creative ideas are not something that live outside you. They are created by you, often lying dormant until you give them a chance to emerge. The ideas from exploration whizz and whirl, forging new configurations—it's up to you to catch them. It matters not whether you prefer to think of yourself as a vessel or a conjurer; you have to allow yourself to receive new ideas when they come.

Legendary comedian John Cleese describes this state of receptivity as the *open mode*. The open mode is the state of being open to new ideas and receptive to what your generative brain offers you. When you are in the open mode, Cleese notes, you notice your thoughts without criticism, you play with them, you improvise and develop. And this is the crux of the creative approach: creative people are open to receiving their ideas.

In generation, you must be willing to receive new ideas as they come to you; even if they're half-formed. It is in the open mode where divergent thinking flourishes. Your usual shield of criticism is down so you can become loose, playful, and silly. Open-ended ventures require a stance of receptivity without rigid objectives.

Most minds want to find this state naturally, but years of closed-mind training comes at a cost. Schools teach the open mode out of us, so we deny ourselves these periods of magic-making. We learn to be editors instead of ideators, analytical instead of imaginative. The open mode is a practised evocation, a learned surrender. The more you get into the open mode, the easier it becomes.

Alfred Hitchcock is regarded as one of the great figures in cinema. When he was on his sets, he and the production team would often get stuck on a problem. They'd usually try and rush to a solution so that they could get back to filming. But Hitchcock had a strange habit in these times. He would stop everyone and mutter, "We're pressing. We're pressing." He would then go on to frustrate his colleagues by telling a rambling story that had nothing to do with the problem at hand.

But Hitchcock knew what he was doing. He understood the creative mind. He mistrusted working under pressure. He intuited that his team was stuck in closed mind loops. By telling his stories, he interrupted the stressed and narrow approaches and invited his crew to loosen into the open mode.

Inevitably, the film team would return to the task with some novel ideas and fresh solutions.

My most vivid experiences with generative creativity and the open mode started at university—as a side project. I had no good model for creativity back then, but I come from a musical family. My father has a deep passion for the guitar, and he instilled in us his love of jazz and soul music. As kids, we would fly off chairs dancing to Luther Vandross. Both of my brothers became professional musicians. I took the more traditional path with actuarial science.

By my university years I'd learnt a bit of guitar but music was more in the background for me. One morning, in reaction to the exacting pressures of my studies, I picked up the guitar and began tinkering. Something clicked, and I wrote a song. It was almost out of the blue: a rough piece with chords and melody and lyrics. I found it utterly intoxicating to be able to sit down and make something up. Although I only learned about this concept of the *open mode* years later, it fits well with my experience of songwriting. I still remember the self-judgement I had to suspend and the fight against the labels I had made for myself. *Permission* is not the right word, but when you don't have experience or deep knowledge in a domain, you struggle with creative licence. I've been writing songs on and off ever since. I do it for only one reason: because I enjoy it. Because of my experience making music and countless other small moments of creativity in my life, I recommend that everyone finds a project where they can get into the open mode more often. Do it for yourself. Play with the infinite elements of a craft, and make something unique. This is how you learn to be generative.

Great improvisation also requires the open mode. When you are improvising, you are responding in the moment. You developed a database of creative ideas in the Exploration phase, and those ideas surface and collide with improvisation. When stage performers like comedians or jazz musicians riff, there is little time for conscious filtering—they play what comes. Improvisation is creativity dancing in the moment; it's a shared experience. You improvise in a meeting coming up with a new idea or process, on the stage when you react to other performers and the crowd, when the light hits your canvas and you see a new colour scheme. Improvisation differs depending on the domain, but you can think of it as live generation, immediate recombination, before the Amelioration phase where there is time to hone the idea. Improvisation is generative creativity in its most raw form—and it is an art that you can get better at. Generation need not always happen behind closed doors in quiet.

The open mode is where you enlist combinatory creativity to keep finding surprise. Surprise is your guide to originality. You must keep recombining ideas until you surprise yourself. Broadly, we can talk about three types of recombination on the road to originality: replicative, incremental, radical.

Replicative creativity entails taking something known and making it your own. Old ideas meet a new style. It's your version or take on an existing work. In music, an example of this would be a cover—a musician plays an existing song in their style. Covers can be highly creative: watch Jimi Hendrix play the "Star-Spangled Banner" for a classic example. Classical musicians are accused of only playing what's there, but we do not see the millions of creative choices with emphasis, pause, volume, and pace. There are endless dimensions for the masters of a field. Replicative creativity is very different from imitation: it's in your style.

Incremental creativity is a kind of creative transformation where the output resembles the previous version, but with significant changes. Vincent van Gogh said, "Great things are done by a series of small things brought together." Think about the iPhone 16, and compare it to the iPhone 5 or 10. Incremental creativity improved the camera, the screen, the memory, the speed, the UX. Incremental creativity builds new elements into existing work. Small inventive changes can dramatically alter the value of the product. So incremental creativity employs iterative development. While still modelled off the original, there has been clear modification or improvement.

Radical creativity is the most original kind of generative creativity. This work yields output unrecognisable from the inputs. Margaret Boden, the late cognitive scientist, conceived of radical creativity as *transformational creativity*. In her words: "Transformational creativity changes the very space of possibilities itself." Radical creativity can create a new domain by writing a new set of rules. This could be a new subfield in science, like with Darwin's theory of evolution by natural selection, or Charlie Parker's development of bebop, or Picasso's cubism. Using a tired cliché, radical creativity is not about thinking outside the box—it's about creating a new box entirely.

To go to a place where you can be generative and find original ideas, you have to give yourself space and time and permission. And when you do, what a thing! Pulling theories and notes and lyrics and stories out of the air; you are making something utterly unique.

Tinkering

As Benjamin Franklin grew older, he faced a common problem: his eyesight was failing. Like many, he needed glasses to read, but he also needed a different prescription to see distant objects clearly. Carrying around two pairs of glasses— one for reading, one for distance—was incredibly frustrating and inconvenient for a busy man who lived to read, write, and conduct experiments.

One day, Franklin had a crazy idea. Instead of switching glasses all the time, what if he combined both lenses into a single pair? He took the two pairs of spectacles and cut the lenses in half. He then crafted a new pair where the top half was for distance vision and the bottom half was for reading. This simple design allowed him to switch focus just by moving his eyes up or down—without swapping glasses.

These "bifocals" were revolutionary. They helped Franklin continue his wide-ranging work without interruption, and soon others adopted the idea. Though he never patented the design (true to his belief that useful inventions should benefit all), Franklin's bifocals endure to this day.

Benjamin Franklin was the ultimate tinkerer. Bifocals are a small part of his creative legacy. He also invented the urinary catheter, the lightning rod, swim fins, and the Franklin stove (to name just a few). In some ways he invented the United States of America as a founding father. Franklin employed a wonderful free-range creativity, and he is my exemplar for the tinkering approach.

Creativity cannot be predicted. Although creative work can be scheduled, what you come up with awaits to be discovered. To unleash generative creativity, you must tinker. The more you experiment and explore, the greater the chance for serendipitous outcomes and fruitful creative accidents. Remember that John Pemberton discovered Coca-Cola while trying to make a medicine for headaches and fatigue.

Open-mindedness and open-endedness are keys to creative flourishing. Tinkering requires a trust that trying things will lead to discovery.

Creative Irreducibility

There is a concept from computer science, coined by the fecund thinker Stephen Wolfram, that is highly relevant to understanding the creative process. This idea is termed *computational irreducibility*. This is a fancy way of describing a certain kind of process with an outcome that is not predictable. In an irreducible process, the end state cannot be known at the start. In other words: the only way to see what happens is to let things unfold. Creativity is such a process.

Creative irreducibility—my new term—says we can never know what our creativity will produce, so we must allow discovery. This is why creativity research emphasises the need for openness. No creative process can be replicated or rerun. Different processes might arrive at similar results, but the process is always as unique as the person or people engaging in it.

In their underrated book *Why Greatness Cannot Be Planned: The Myth of the Objective*, computer scientists Kenneth Stanley and Joel Lehman take a computational approach to outline the open-endedness and irreducibility of the creative process. They proved why you cannot know in advance what will be discovered. You make progress with smaller goals. Line by line, character by character, note by note, idea by idea.

Creative irreducibility is seen across fields. Scientists, for example, come up with new conjectures in unpredictable ways. The academy does not progress neatly from one theory to the next. Science—like art and business and everything else—is subject to random discoveries, serendipity, chance. Theory does not necessarily lead to new tools, invention does.

The author Nassim Taleb got me onto the idea that few of the memorable inventions in history came about from scientists with set objectives. Warfarin was meant to be a rat poison, not a life-saving blood thinner; Viagra was meant to treat chest pain; the pacemaker was initially built to monitor heart sounds, not regulate the heartbeat. Most people think that science and technology follow a linear path of progress. The history of ideas shows us that this just ain't so. The evolution of culture follows a winding and intractable path. Wherever you look—construction, medicine, physics, energy—much of the progress came from unpredictable discoveries.

Generative tinkerers are primed to notice interesting new patterns when they arise. Louis Pasteur said that chance favours the prepared mind. You must embrace the tinkering approach in your own work: do the technical work and then have the willingness to pivot, and the appetite to follow surprise. It does not matter in which field, be it business, science, or art, genuinely creative people can't help but tinker.

Every creative session is an opportunity to tinker and experiment. In this formulation creativity encourages failure. Inventor James Dyson built a technology empire on the spirit of experimentation. His invention of the bagless vacuum cleaner came after thousands of prototypes and countless failed attempts. Dyson viewed each failed invention as a vital piece of feedback, learning something new every time a design did not work. His relentless tinkering, and openness to failure, allowed him to break free from traditional constraints and invent valuable new products. One of the joys in creative work is finding solutions you weren't expecting.

We have these fizzing, bubbling, generative minds. If you harness your mental effervescence and go where the day takes you, you might arrive somewhere truly inspired. You want to foster intentional accidents. This is why you can't be too rigid about the outcomes you hope for. Missteps are part of the process; detours can be welcome.

Rules of the Game

In part 2, we talk about embracing constraints to be generative. The rules of a creative domain are your primary and most necessary constraint. Without rules you cannot define a domain. Without rules you have no foothold into a field. But when held too rigidly, rules can limit imagination.

Young people do great work when they aren't fully aware of the rules they have to follow. They aren't inhibited by an overfamiliar structure. In some fields, like those in science, progress is impossible without some grasp of the rules—the current theories. You might have heard the advice: "Learn the rules so that you can break them." In other fields, the sooner you start playing with the rules the better. Starting early leaves you unencumbered by the arbitrary limits of others. Orson Welles recounts how he innovated in his movies from a place of sheer ignorance. He didn't know the old rules of filmmaking, so he made up his own. Welles said,

> I thought you could do anything with a camera that the eye could do, or the imagination could do. And if you come up from the bottom in the film business, you're taught all the things that the cameraman doesn't want to attempt for fear he will be criticised for having failed. And in this case, I had a cameraman who didn't care if he was criticised if he failed, and I didn't know that there were things you couldn't do. So anything I could think up in my dreams, I attempted to photograph.

The inimitable Immanuel Kant said, "Genius is a talent for producing something for which no determinate rule can be given, not a predisposition consisting of a skill for something that can be learned by following some rule or other: hence the foremost property of genius must be originality." If exploration is about learning the rules, generation is about playing within these rules—sometimes breaking them or creating new rules entirely (transformational creativity). When your work becomes fuzzier, less defined, slightly uncomfortable, you may be onto something.

In 1941, Miles Davis was fifteen and already playing trumpet with a seriousness that scared people. He didn't play fast like Dizzy. He didn't shout like Louis. He played slow. Sparse. Like each note mattered more than the rest.

He studied at Juilliard, but skipped classes to haunt 52nd Street, listening to Charlie Parker blow apart the old world of jazz. Bebop was wild and fast and brilliant. Miles joined in—but even then, he held back. Space, not speed, became his language.

Then came 1959. Kind of Blue. *No rehearsals. No sheet music. Just sketches—modes, not chords. A suggestion of harmony. Miles told the band: "Play it like you don't know what comes next." That album changed everything.*

It wasn't about complexity. It was about possibility. With fewer rules, more could happen. Every track was a doorway. Every solo a walk into the unknown.

Miles never stayed still. When the world caught up to one sound, he'd burn it down and start over with a new set of rules. Cool jazz. Modal jazz. Fusion. Electronics. Silence.

"Don't play what's there," he said. "Play what's not there."

Infinite Spaces

The famed Argentine writer Jorge Luis Borges wrote a short story titled *The Library of Babel* where he conceived of an infinite library. This conceptual library has never-ending shelves that house every possible combination of every book.

Borges writes of his library:

> The universe (which others call the Library) is composed of an indefinite and perhaps infinite number of hexagonal galleries with vast air shafts between, surrounded by very low railings. From any one of the hexagons one can see, interminably, the upper and lower floors. The distribution of the galleries is invariable. Twenty shelves, five long shelves per side, cover all the sides except two; their height, which is the distance from floor to ceiling, scarcely exceeds that of a normal bookcase.

This boundless library is a beautiful metaphor for creative work and potential. Libraries are made up of books with letters; these are the creative constituents. Every configuration of letters is possible, from garbage strings of text to Shakespeare. The infinite library is a space of vast possibilities, in both search and discovery.

Borges Space

The Borges Library is but one of an endless number of creative spaces. I term the space of possibility in each creative domain the *Borges Space*. The Possibility Space, the Borges Space, contains all the configurations of creative work in that realm, from gibberish to the sublime. The rules of the domain distinguish between different types of Borges Spaces.

Borges had his library; but a different type of Borges Space might be of interest to painters: a Borges Gallery holds every conceivable painting. A Borges Studio contains every song that is possible to record.

Borges Spaces are as diverse as our culture, expanding and contracting with our collective ingenuity and categorisations. There are Borges Spaces to consider wherever you look, ready to be engaged: Libraries, Studios, Gardens, Laboratories, Companies, Galleries, Kitchens. You can define these spaces in your own way. Indeed, unique points of view take you deeper into richer configurations of the space. There is a Borges Space for whatever type of work interests you.

Creative work involves play within and across these Borges Spaces. The MEGA framework benefits from the Borges Space (Possibility Space) concept in each phase. Motivation is about choosing the kind of Borges Space you want to play in. Exploration is about engaging with the rules of that space, learning the current configurations. Generation is about discovering new possibilities in the space through recombination. Amelioration is about honing these discoveries to best match your problems, selecting the best version of what you've discovered.

Creative life offers a Rolodex of Possibility Spaces. Picking your domain is the work of motivation. In the figure below, Possibility Space is shown in two dimensions, but really every creative domain has infinite dimensions, infinite elements to tweak and recombine. Each different component in a creative work takes you in a different direction, to a different configuration.

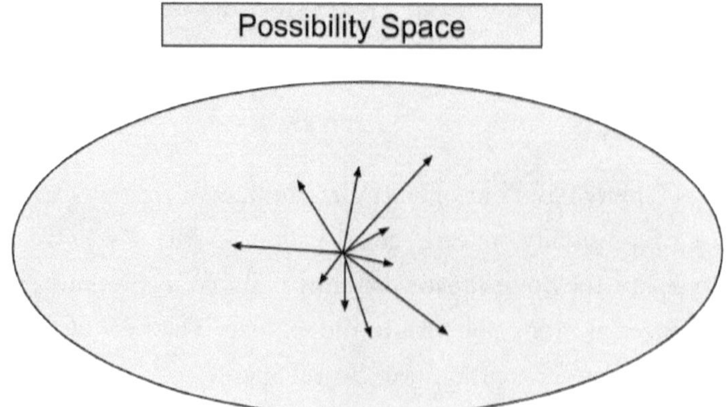

Take the example of writing a song. You have infinite options as you start out. Think of all the elements: the feel, the riff, the style, the lyrics, the length, the form, the chords, the instruments, the melody, the breaks, the beat. The Borges Song is multidimensional; the area for variation is practically infinite. Each element is a new direction in Possibility Space. As you make creative choices, you move towards more specific parts of the Borges Space until you consolidate and configure a new idea—a new song, in this case. You'll notice the songs neighbouring this idea are very similar with minor variations, depending on which element you vary.

Search and Discovery

Possibility Space requires search and discovery. In the Exploration phase, we spoke about the *Search Space* where discovery meant the discovery of old ideas. This was the search for good ideas already crystallised in the world. This exploratory creativity entailed finding the good ideas that have already been discovered and determining those most relevant for your creative plans.

At the ends of Search Space, the *Discovery Space* begins. The Search Space and the Discovery Space are complementary subsets in the space of possibility, yin and yang. In the Generation phase, we use the current ideas from our explorations as footholds to climb into the void of uncertainty. Generative creativity is about recombining old ideas into new configurations, thereby unleashing ideas previously undiscovered. We configure new ideas into being with our generative creativity. These ideas always existed in theory, but until they are discovered they do not exist in reality. Creativity propels us through the realm of possibilities.

New ideas are usually formed close to existing ideas—because new solutions contain antecedent ideas recombined. The ideas sampled in the Exploration phase are the creator's stepping stones in the Generation phase. To form new ideas, generative creativity actualises new realms of the Discovery Space. As soon as new ideas are discovered, once they crystallise and cool, they become current ideas and move into the Search Space.

Search leads to discovery. In the work of generation, one new idea leads to the next: unlocking new possibilities entirely. We spoke about how you must start with the known. In the Exploration phase you tread upon familiar ground, assimilating. In the Generative Space you take steps into the frightful unknown. Bit by bit, you tame infinity. You recombine old ideas, you bring in new contexts, and you make small derivations or large imaginative leaps. These are the steps to original work. The great leaps in Discovery Space require extraordinary effort, special techniques, or lots of luck.

People love to ask if art or maths are invented or discovered. The question does not make sense. Invention is discovery. Discovery is invention.

It is a mathematical fact that the Search Space subset must always be an infinitesimal fraction of the greater set of possibilities available. The preponderance of possibility is always on the horizon. Any Possibility Space holds the wonder of limitless discovery. Think about the undiscovered infinite: the paintings, the mathematical equations, the theories, the inventions. These beckoning, beautiful, daunting spaces await every creatively engaged person. Without a good guide, you will languish in a shallow pool of infinity, never getting deeper yet haunted by the brilliant potential of new ideas just out of reach.

Not every idea is created equal. One cannot navigate the Borges Space with artistic and cultural relativism; you will quickly find yourself unmoored. You navigate by staying close to what is already valued and then venture out, guided by your taste and by what surprises or delights you.

In the Borges Library, the vast preponderance of the books are gibberish. You cannot select works at random. How you navigate a creative space like writing is informed by the work you've done before, by the books you've read, and by the ideas you're currently thinking about. In the Exploration phase, you've looked at what constitutes quality. Now you must develop your nose through generative work of your own. As you wade further out from the known configurations, this challenge grows more difficult but also more exciting.

It's a Kind of Magic

Oliver Sacks referred to our generative creativity as the "buzzing, blooming chaos of the mind." Einstein called it "combinatorial play." Stephen Jay Gould and Steve Jobs thought of it simply as "connecting dots." We cite daemons, muses, vessels, complex brain chemistry—each of us has a different philosophy of creativity.

Creativity is the fantastical act of creating new ideas from old ones. Nothing comes from nothing, but generative creativity can look like magic. Because we don't fully understand how creativity works or how it evolved precisely, we can only marvel at our powers.

At the Walt Disney company, they use the wonderful term *imagineering*. Imagineers come up with new rides at the parks, new toys, and new stories for the Disney universe. Generative creativity is the work of applied imagination. There is a lot of work before and after, but getting to new ideas is a core requirement of creativity.

Einstein said, "if the first idea is not absurd, there is no hope for it." This pairs well with a saying in creative work: "refuse the first solution." Sometimes originality is found on the tenth, the hundredth, the thousandth idea. Divergent thinking is difficult and cognitively demanding, and it requires a certain environment to thrive.

Generation happens in bursts. You cannot control when you'll have new ideas. When you're exploring, a past idea will collide with your current observation. When you're editing, something original might strike. When you're resting, your unconscious will offer you things out of the blue. Ideas will hit you like hail as the heavens open. You must be ready. Seneca said that luck is when preparation meets opportunity. This is why you must always be ready: carry a notebook, use phone apps, waiter pads, anything. Why not collect the harvest you've sowed in your previous sessions? In the Exploration phase you record what you notice, and in the Generation phase you capture what spills out of you.

If you invite the open mode regularly, part of your unconscious brain stays there. As you go about your day, the ideas do not stop percolating. Inspiration and delayed new insights find you at odd hours. This is a direct result from your earlier creative exertion. You must be ready to catch these latecomer sparks.

Creativity is a kind of magic. We are all witches and wizards, if we choose to be. We can enter these vast domains, these spaces of possibility, and discover things no one else has thought about. Of course, it takes a tremendous amount of work and luck before you get to the good stuff, but that's not the point—the point is to make magic.

CHAPTER 4: AMELIORATION

Creative Selection – Convergence – Evaluation – Execution

It's not the notes you play, it's the notes you don't play.

—Miles Davis

Creativity is a wild mind and a disciplined eye.

—Dorothy Parker

Amelioration is the colour of fraying yellow notepads, of revision, of hard work and sweat-stained shirts. Amelioration is defined as *making something better*. It's the phase of iterating and improving, feedback and criticism. It's the phase of finishing and sharing your work.

Amelioration can be thought of as solution selection: evaluating, elaborating, and refining your work. Honing is a great word to describe what you do in the Amelioration phase: shaping works, crafting, a kind of creative selection. Often the Amelioration phase requires reduction—convergence after the generative divergent phase. You will need to kill the darling ideas that don't serve you. Many generative artists, and indeed most people, have no trouble coming up with ideas, but they struggle to polish and reduce. They eschew the hard work of editing and honing. Creativity, if you recall our definition, is about getting to ideas and work that are not only novel *but useful as well as fully developed*.

Too few artists finish projects; too few business plans make it off the page. Amelioration evolves your work and nurtures it into the real world: iterating and adapting the form until it is the best it can be. This is very often the "hard work" or perspiration part of the process. It's the work that involves cleaning the draft, polishing the composition, or making the peer-review edits. This phase involves painful selection and evaluation; it's why many artists avoid it and then struggle to make an impact with their work. It also involves the vulnerability of asking for an audience.

Scientific work progresses with conjecture and criticism. Conjecture of new explanations maps perfectly to the Generation phase. Amelioration then contains the counterbalance of criticism. If generation is ideation, amelioration is execution. It's how you bring ideas to life: in proper context and order, adapted to your problem, fit to share with the world. If generation is hot; amelioration is cold. There are many well-worn descriptions to capture the two active modes of creative work: generation versus amelioration, gut versus brain, heart versus head, feeling versus thinking, open mode versus closed. Some say it differently: "Write drunk, edit sober."

Creative Selection

In his landmark 1964 talk titled "The Creative Personality," Professor Donald MacKinnon at Berkeley says that creativity must fulfil at least three conditions. The first two conditions we have discussed: a creative solution must exhibit originality and usefulness (which align to our previous definition, "new ideas that add value").

MacKinnon's third condition is interesting. He says:

> True creativity involves evaluation and elaboration of the original insight. A sustaining and a developing of it to the full. What I am suggesting is that creativity is a process with a time dimension and which involves adaptiveness, and realisation. It may be brief like the jam session of a jazz band, or it may involve a considerable span of years as was required with Darwin's development or creation of the theory of evolution.

The work of the Amelioration phase is this evaluation and elaboration, the development and realisation of your solution. Original insights require further development. All creative work is about selection. But amelioration is the final phase of selection, where you must select the best of what you have and forge the finished product.

Evolution

Our world changes with evolution: physical, biological, cultural. Creativity is the force of cultural evolution. In biological evolution via natural selection, mutation provides the novel genetic expressions that nature selects for. In cultural evolution via creative selection, exploration and generation provide the new ideas that we select from. This selection occurs in the Amelioration phase. We generate parts of the solution and choose the best pieces to form new solutions.

Evolution in creative work progresses with iteration. The first iteration of something is often ugly. What you produce in the Generation phase is rarely ready to publish. Stories need reworking, songs need remixing, business products need updates. "Bohemian Rhapsody" was unrecognisable and unplayable on the first take. The first websites of big tech firms like Google and Airbnb were famously ugly. The first draft of *The Great Gatsby* was weak in narrative and structure. Amelioration is the phase of improvement via new iteration.

Great works go through endless rounds of revision. In projects, this is an evolution of sorts. With each revision, each layer, the work changes and takes better shape. There are exceptions of course, but most projects will need many rounds of editing and revision before they are ready to be released.

Keep reworking with your ideal reader in mind. What would they like? What is unnecessary? J. R. R. Tolkien said, "Little by little, one travels far." It's been said that Tolkien spent several decades honing the fictional world of Middle-earth, the setting for *The Lord of the Rings.* Bit by bit he built a whole new world. This took endless revision. He invented languages, mythology, peoples, events. Great works evolve with the sweat of amelioration.

Each iteration can bring you closer to great work or take you further away. We'll talk later about how feedback and criticism can give you guidance. But before this, you must follow your nose and allow for multiple versions of your work to exist in Possibility Space before you select your favourite.

Taste

You might ask: How does one make creative selections? The answer is taste. Call it judgement, critical evaluation, creative discretion—it's all part of your developing sense of taste. Taste is the key to ameliorative work. It is hard-won, but it accumulates, and then it snowballs and compounds. As you raise your bar in one sphere, you see the potential for craft and process in all.

You need some level of immersion before your taste develops properly. Ira Glass once said that "when you start, your taste outpaces your ability." That gap is painful—but it's proof of potential.

Taste in this sense is *judgement tuned by experience*. And like judgement, it improves with feedback, exposure, and failure. You develop taste by seeing more and caring more—by consuming widely, revising ruthlessly, and comparing your instincts to the output of the masters. It's slow work. But over time, you start to hear it: the internal *click* when something lands right.

You must trust yourself. It's all you can do. Creativity writer Austin Kleon says, "Draw the art you want to see, start the business you want to run, play the music you want to hear, write the books you want to read, build the products you want to use—do the work you want to see done."

Taste is a crucial part of ameliorative creativity. If the generative phase is a striking storm of possibilities, taste is the still hand that selects, edits, and refines. Raymond Carver wrote stories that seem spare and simple but were whittled down over dozens of revisions. His taste leaned towards restraint.

Taste is especially critical in open-ended domains like writing, music, design—in the spaces where infinite configurations are possible. There's no formula. You can't muscle through the choices with brute force. You need taste—hard-won creative judgement—to prune the tree of possibilities down to a single branch.

You know you're developing good taste when poor-quality works in your domain offend you. You notice where a bit of creativity, care, and craft could have made something better. When you develop a nose for quality, you look for it in other fields as well. Taste is transferrable in this way.

As you improve your skills, the quality of your generation improves. The more time you devote to your craft in the other phases, the easier you will find the Amelioration phase. If you have a strong sense of what your work should look like, the work of refining is easier: it's clear what does and does not belong.

The Amelioration phase, through creative selection, is where you develop your style. Style is the unique way in which you operate in your field, and it's informed by your taste. You develop unique moves and an original voice. From taste, style flows. Roberta Flack said, "I've been told I sound like Nina Simone, Nancy Wilson, Odetta, Barbra Streisand, Dionne Warwick, even Mahalia Jackson. If everybody said I sounded like one person, I'd worry. But when they say I sound like them all, I know I've got my own style."

Convergence

Steve Jobs said it takes a lot of hard work to make something simple. There is great craft in reducing something to its most elegant, simple, and essential form.

If generation was about divergence, amelioration is about convergence. You collected dots in exploration, connected them in generation, now in amelioration you must carefully select the right dots and remove the dots that do not serve your solution.

This final phase of the creative process entails production by reduction, addition by subtraction. Once the ideas are generated, it's time to hone, taking the best of what you have, into the right form, and in the correct order. You must whittle down to the final product. This requires stripping and reshaping your work with love: honouring the initial idea and the art form.

Rick Rubin is a fabulously successful record producer. He likes to talk about himself as a "reducer." He claims his only talent is his taste. He guides musicians to their core sound, to what makes the song special. Ed Sheeran, Red Hot Chili Peppers, Adele, Eminem, Tom Petty, Johnny Cash, Jay-Z—everyone wants to work with him. Clearly Rubin understands something about the creative process; he wrote a book of collected thoughts called *The Creative Act*. On the work of amelioration, he says this: "Whereas the Experimentation phase is about what the seed has to offer, now we are applying our filter."

I've always liked that old Michelangelo quote about sculpting. When asked how he created one of his masterpieces, he said: "I created a vision of David in my mind and simply carved away everything that was not David." Pair this with Picasso who said that art is the elimination of the unnecessary. Amelioration is this art of honing.

After the heat of the Generation phase, you want to cool down. Once you're sitting with the output of generation, you need to edit with ice in your veins. No emotional attachment to beautiful text that does not fit the story, no saving the chord-heavy bridge that does not serve your song, and no room for experimental evidence that does not support your theory.

You must be a killer in the final phase of creative work, cutting the very things you have lovingly created. Stephen King says, "Kill your darlings." Bruce Lee says, "Hack away at the unessential." Effective revision is surgical. Creative aspirants become creative professionals when they can do the difficult work of cold-blooded reduction.

Steven Pinker, speaking on writing, reflects on how the presence of a word count often elevates his prose. Removing unnecessary words in your piece is a kindness to the reader. Brevity clarifies your message and improves your style.

Elegance

Da Vinci said simplicity is the ultimate sophistication. After you remove the unnecessary parts of your work, you notice the beauty of simplicity. Default to simplicity over complexity. Elegance is the hidden architecture of great creative work—it's what makes something *feel* inevitable once it exists.

The generative stage is messy, explosive, filled with digressions and excess. Elegance is found in the sculpting. Elegance is not always the absence of ornament; it's when each element earns its place. When nothing can be added or taken away without breaking the whole. In mathematics, elegance is often what distinguishes a merely correct proof from a beautiful one. A great example is Euler's formula: $e^{i\pi} + 1 = 0$; there is nothing superfluous. Elegance is both guide and destination. In design, think of the original iPod click wheel. It combined input and navigation into a single intuitive gesture. It made something complex feel easy.

When you unlock the right form for your creative work, surprising things happen. When you find the right structure for the book, suddenly you know where to hang your new ideas. When you discover a new form for your song, the right chords and lyrics reveal themselves. Elegance elevates your work.

Evaluation

Each year, Louis C. K. throws out his act and begins with fresh material. When he explains to other comedians how he develops the new material from scratch, their faces darken and they go speechless. Then they ask: All of it?

C. K. throws out every part of his act except the last bit, which he starts his next show with. Comedians always close with the best bits of their act. That means that each new show must outperform the best part of his previous hour. Chris Rock, when he heard that C. K. did this, said: "That's how you got so good, man."

In preparation for a new special, C. K. takes to the road, playing new bits in many settings and different audiences. He is constantly reworking the material. The instant feedback from the audience tells the comedian what to focus on, what to emphasise, what to cut, and what to keep.

Evaluation is an art. Learning how to find, accept, and apply criticism and feedback will lift the quality of your work. The process of evaluation is internal and external: First you critique your own work, then you must seek feedback.

Creativity Quotient

As you bring your ideas into the world and shape your work with feedback and the throbbing noise of criticism, try not to lose the essence of your craft. Never forget the core requirements for your creative domain. Painters need to paint well. Writers must write legibly. Legendary stand-up Norm MacDonald said, "Comedians should be funny."

Keep working on your own style, but remember the form. In each field there are functional requirements: don't skip the basics. Businesses must turn a profit, science must advance knowledge, artists must challenge with expression, dancers must dance. In amelioration, you must go back to basics when you critically assess the work. Be careful of the sideshows and keep the main thing the main thing.

To evaluate the output of your creative work, you can use something I term the *creativity quotient*. The creativity quotient is the criterion you can use for creative criticism. A quotient is defined as *the degree or amount of a specified quality or characteristic.*

Creative output, in the standard definition, has two important dimensions: novelty and usefulness. If something is both novel and useful, in context, it must also be valuable. Value is what we are after. The creativity quotient is the degree to which creative output is useful and novel—shown in four quadrants in the graph below. Something is increasingly valuable as you move to the top and to the right. The more useful and original, the more valuable.

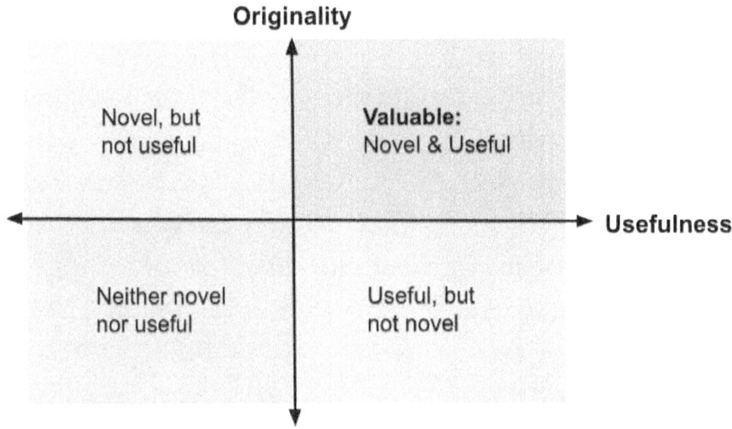

How different is your output from your inputs? How close are other solutions to your problem? Something can be novel to you and known by others. Creativity researcher Margaret Boden spoke about *psychological creativity* and *historical creativity*. Psychological creativity occurs when you discover something that is novel and useful to you. But historical creativity occurs when you are the first person to offer that valuable idea.

While there will always be a degree of subjectivity when assessing a work and a need for understanding the context of the problem, most solutions can be analysed with the creativity quotient. Some problems are harder than others. Some solutions are more ingenious, more inventive, more detailed than others. Great solutions, like the works of Da Vinci or Einstein, have very high creativity quotients. It is not always necessary to compare, but a work benefits from being critically evaluated while it is being shaped.

Creative work has no inherent morality; you, as the creator, must decide if you're doing good work. The above graph of the creativity quotient misses this crucial element of moral consideration. In different contexts, something could be valuable or harming. Work you find valuable can have positive or negative impact in the world. Nuclear power generates energy for millions but also threatens global extinction with atomic warheads. Creative advance is often double-edged, and its usefulness depends on the moral framework and the context of use.

Lastly, I would recommend a different type of criticism from evaluating output. This layer of evaluation is more of a check-in for yourself, and in some ways it is a return to motivation. Put output aside for a moment, and ask: Are you enjoying yourself? Is your self-talk positive? Does the work give you purpose? Are you being too critical of yourself? We can often be incredibly unkind to ourselves if we are not meeting an expected standard. This kind of evaluation is on the process rather than the product. Before proceeding with criticism of output, see that you are still creating with a positive mindset and that the process is still aligned to the values and work to which you aspire.

The ultimate guide for your work is your own nose: Is this something you want to see in the world? That's all you can do: keep making more of the things you want to see in the world.

Feedback

You've laboured to produce a work. You've arrived at an original premise. You've toiled and honed the work. Your piece is close to finished, and you're almost happy. What now? Now you need to share it. Find a friend to read your draft. Publish your video to a limited audience. Release the work into the wild. You must seek criticism. Finding valid feedback is an essential part of the Amelioration phase. The second part of criticism, after self-evaluation, is getting feedback.

There are some rules of engagement. First, and sadly, the world does not care about you particularly. There is something worse than bad feedback: no feedback. It is very likely that no one cares about your project. Do not be put off by cold indifference—it's up to you to get people's attention. You can be creative about finding feedback or become so good that they can't ignore you (more on this later). But even mastery will not guarantee you an audience. Sharing your work effectively requires a different set of skills. You can develop these yourself, or outsource them, but an inability to share your work will cost you great opportunities for collaboration, peer review, and the chance to elevate the work.

I've heard it said that half the work is making your thing, and the other half is getting it out into the world. Part of the process is to make people notice, if only to get feedback. Without feedback you'll never truly know what you have. Sometimes the world is not receptive to your work, for many reasons. If you don't get the reaction you want, it may not be due to the quality of your work. It could be that your reviewer was distracted. Something else could have been happening that day. Perhaps the mood and timing were not right.

Many people like to get feedback early on. They like to test if they are on the right path. But there are good reasons to wait before you share. The creative ego is fragile. A few careless words can kill momentum in generation; you must protect fledgling ideas until they can stand on their own legs. Form your work properly before you test it. But when you feel your work is close to being ready, get it into the world.

Prepare yourself, because reality gives harsh feedback. Expect it; look forward to it. Relish the review that makes you better. Marvel that someone cares enough to critique you. You don't exist in isolation, so your creativity must make contact with the world. You can't be too thin-skinned. Skip the sensitive artist phase. Discuss your work! Expect judgement. Most people are secretly ashamed that they are not in any creative arena, and they will scoff at the attempts of others. But remember that you tried—you battled, you laboured to make something in this world and make something of yourself. If you fail, there is no shame. Try, and try again. Your struggle is to balance feedback without eroding your confidence.

Sometimes feedback should be ignored. J. K. Rowling was rejected twelve times when presenting *Harry Potter* to publishers. Winning original work will not always be recognised as such, and not all criticism is valid.

There are levels of value. Something can be useful to you only. Something can be valuable to your community. Something can be valuable to the world. The definition of usefulness varies by field and setting. Formal domains have gatekeepers. Usually these institutional players assess whether a new set of ideas or products will become influential. Increasingly, the role of gatekeepers is diminishing as access to markets opens with the internet and a globalised world. In some fields, like academia, you still need to publish and undergo peer review if your ideas are to be validated. In the arts it's becoming easier and easier to share your work and let your audience decide if they like it—and if they do, it's considered valuable.

Generally, the tighter the definition of work in a domain, the easier it is to judge value. Mathematics, for example, is a well-defined space. A good mathematician can very quickly tell you if you have a valid new proof or an interesting line of inquiry that says something new or useful. Psychology, on the other hand, is far messier and more ambiguous. When the rules and progress metrics of the field are harder to define, it's far more difficult to assess if you've achieved usefulness.

The subjectivity in domains like business and art necessitates a simpler feedback criterion: create value for the people who engage with your work. In business, a new product is valuable if it solves a problem for someone. In art, a piece is useful if someone finds beauty in it and they want to engage with it or purchase it.

Sometimes you must bend the world to come around to your ideas. This takes a lot of doing. Do not compromise on the things that make your work special if these are your points of creative difference. If the feedback is such that you doubt your whole enterprise, make sure this has been confirmed by multiple valid sources. Even then, you might still have a unique vision. When you really believe in something, you can bring others around with your passion or through the quality of what you are producing. If your work receives negative feedback for sustained periods by multiple sources, then perhaps reassess.

Trust your taste, develop your discernment, and learn to take criticism. Find a hunger for valid criticism, especially from people who you respect. Great criticism is a creative act by your reviewer, and negative feedback is a gift. Someone has taken time to tell you how you can be better. After a while, you'll come to dislike generic compliments because they don't make you better. If you care for your craft and want to improve, then you want the most honest review.

Execution

Celebrity psychologist Adam Grant says, "Creativity is abundant. Execution is scarce." In my conception, execution is part of the creative process. People can't help but have ideas, but execution is the work of turning good ideas into finished works.

The great scientist Michael Faraday said the secret to creative progress is simple—three words: *work, finish, publish*. Total creativity demands the difficult final steps of finishing and publishing. These last pieces in the Amelioration phase require clinical execution. Executing a creative vision is not included in most people's definition of creativity. It should be. Without the savvy application of amelioration, your output is half-baked, novel without necessarily being useful, forever unfinished and unappreciated.

Finish

For years after I finished high school, I wanted to write more. I didn't have an outlet. I wasn't a "writer." I had drafts and ideas, but no completed pieces. As I said in the introduction, during the twilight zone of the coronavirus pandemic, I started a blog and began posting finished pieces online. As you might imagine, my early pieces were not particularly good—but I always figured a bad writer is still a writer. The leap to action was the blog. I had to finish a piece before I could post it. Every time I hit publish, my work went into the world.

I was finally finishing pieces and sharing them. I was executing. I cannot emphasise this step enough. There is a vast chasm of creative learning between a draft in a desk drawer and a finished essay mailed to people's inboxes. The draft in my drawer was a set of unfulfilled ideas; the published essay was a creative product. It takes the mindset of amelioration to finish and share your work.

Much of what this book has to say about creativity is generalisable; for any person, any field, any project, any problem. In general, it's a good idea to finish your projects. But this is not true for every person, every field, every project, every problem. There are many cases where "aim to finish" is very bad advice.

Imagine someone told J. R. R. Tolkien, while he spent decades developing his masterwork in Middle-earth, to "finish up." Sometimes great works need an unreasonable amount of time.

Publish

At some point your project will hit an inflection point. The work will enter a stage where marginal improvements become exceedingly difficult and time intensive. The opportunity cost of small improvements in your current project versus the benefits of starting a new project becomes increasingly difficult to justify. This is where the "good-enough rule" must be considered. *Done is better than perfect.* This philosophy will drive action in your creative life.

There are so many projects you can work on, it might be time to move on from your current one. Every project is different, and each individual's standards are different—my "good enough" may not pass your muster. Sometimes your work must sit and breathe before you return to it. Sometimes you can work in a fiery fervour and publish quickly. It depends on your field, on your temperament, and on your ambitions. Aim to finish the projects that matter. And when you're finished, share your work. Like everything we do, creativity is social. Get your ideas out there. It's more fun that way too.

We've come to the end of part 1. I hope you have found some value in the MEGA model of the creative process. Part 2 looks at the process behind the work: the mindset and psychology of creative work, the elements of a creative practice, and the protocols to keep working well.

PART 2:
MEGA TOOLS

How to be more creative.

CHAPTER 5: PSYCHOLOGY

Creative Traits – Mindset – Resilience

The worst enemy to creativity is self-doubt.

—Sylvia Plath

Before we can discuss the practices and protocols that will unlock your creative process, we should first look at the psychology of creativity. How do your beliefs influence the work you do? Do you have a mindset that embraces creative change? The biggest obstacle you face in your battle to be more creative is yourself. Are you able to master your time, muster your discipline, and get to work? We tell ourselves all sorts of negative things, like we're not creative, we're not good enough, the work we do is not creative, or our work is not worth sharing. So of course we procrastinate, and isolate, and lament.

The psychology of creativity is complex. We must deal with creative struggle, battles with confidence, and the dangerous idea of identity. In this chapter we look at traits, mindset, emotional resilience, and how the creative mind can be liberated. Your potential is partly constrained by your ideas about yourself and how you manage your emotions.

The first part of this book was intended to offer a new framework for creative work. But how you think about yourself has massive impact on what you'll do. If you do not attach self-worth to every project, you will try more things and take more risks. If you're motivated intrinsically, you're likely to enjoy yourself more. If you learn to tolerate uncertainty, you will find more surprises. The potential to live creatively or do interesting work depends on what kind of person you are and how you work with your unique psychology. Some traits are fixed, and others you can change with time. With therapy, introspection, or good systems, you can manage negative self-talk and creative blocks. By practising openness, scheduling novelty-seeking, and cultivating a playful mindset, you can cultivate greater creativity in your life.

Creative Traits

In his book, *Creativity: Flow and the Psychology of Discovery and Invention*, psychologist Mihaly Csikszentmihalyi looked at nearly a hundred high-achieving individuals across varied creative domains. The study included jazz great Oscar Peterson, celebrated biologist and author Stephen Jay Gould, double Nobel Prize winner Linus Pauling, astronomer Vera Rubin, and many others.

After interviewing these creative luminaries, Csikszentmihalyi searched for the traits and approaches that united his subjects. What he found surprised him. His first general observation was that the great creatives he studied tended to have a natural predisposition for the work of their domain. They found their curiosity bull's-eye: work matched to their intellectual or sensory advantages. Second, the creative minds he interviewed all ranked very highly on openness to experience. This is an attitude to learning and creating that is intertwined with curiosity. Similar to what we discussed in chapter 2, "Exploration," Csikszentmihalyi also concluded that openness and curiosity are essential attitudes for creative success.

In terms of personalities, they were more different than they were similar. The overarching theme was complexity: highly creative people have a dynamic range of psychological traits. Top creative minds are hard to categorise as they are exceptionally adaptable. Csikszentmihalyi found several paradoxical personality pairs that creative minds manage to navigate between: playful and disciplined, imaginative and realistic, rebellious and conservative, energetic and restful, passionate and objective. The remarkable thing was that the participants exhibited the ability to adopt the right mode when the work required it. When they needed to open their Possibility Spaces, they could activate playfulness and energy; when they needed to hone skills or edit, they showed aptitude for discipline and objectivity.

It is refreshing and remarkable that creative minds are messy in that they need not be defined in one way. Whatever your dominant traits, you can cultivate the opposing trait. If you tend to conservatism, your creative practice can encourage more freedom and rebellious thinking. If you are wildly imaginative, you might invite realism to constrain you with more consideration of the practical. The creative mind is agile, and when applied to the right work, you just might find new aptitudes and ways of thinking that will surprise you. From the psychological literature, we can glean a few pieces of advice: find the work that suits you; cultivate an open curiosity; and facilitate a more flexible approach when the work requires it.

Mindset

Identity is a powerful thing. It's formed by where you come from and by what you believe. People's identities are illustrated in what they do. Narrow identities limit exploration and growth. When you think you're a certain kind of person, your activities are limited to that definition. This can help you focus, but it might also stop you from exploring and trying new things. Anchoring your identity with a craft or a calling is a compelling strategy in a world of overwhelming options. The labels of "writer," "entrepreneur," "scientist," or "musician" can steer your wandering mind back to work. These systems of identity can aid you when motivation ebbs—but if you wear your identities lightly, your potential may expand.

In my student days, a book by psychologist Carol Dweck made a great impression on me. The book is *Mindset: The New Psychology of Success*. The essential idea is that people hold themselves back with fixed mindsets. They have rigid parameters of their potential, and this stops them trying things and changing their lives with more agency. On the other side of the mindset spectrum, Dweck talks about people who cultivate *growth mindsets*. Such people are not so tethered to a fixed identity; they believe in agency, in the ability to learn across domains and problem types. Most critically, growth mindsets are found in people who believe they can improve their abilities.

Of course, no amount of belief or mental training is going to give you the wingspan of Michael Phelps, the intellect of John von Neumann, or the ear of Stevie Wonder. The growth mindset only works when your aptitude and natural proclivities are matched to the work you choose. If you want to master the creative work in question, it's best to have realistic goals according to your natural limits. Pairing these goals with a growth mindset will take you to interesting places.

Resilience

Creativity has a dark side. Our wild imaginations make us suffer. The agency bestowed by new options can drive us to great anxiety. The work can be lonely and frustrating. Obsession threatens relationships. Failure is common. In many cases, creative work goes unacknowledged. History is replete with stories of great artists who lived in squalor.

You cannot separate your creative work from the rest of your life. If you are struggling, you will struggle to work. Sometimes the work is the cause of the stress, but often the work can be a place of solace and recharge. Many people use their creativity to cope, citing art or music as therapy. Fiction teaches empathy. Gardening invites calm. Doing meaningful work gives people a sense of achievement and purpose, and many use their creativity to feel better about the world despite the setbacks they face. Creative minds do amazing things when put to work, but they become anxious if they do not find release valves. Creative engagement is a channel for our emotions. Certain negative emotions—like grief—can act as further fuel for artistic expression, can strengthen resolve, or can deepen the emotional resonance of a work. Quincy Jones lost his mother to schizophrenia and dementia. She spent most of his childhood in an institution. Jones said he made "music his mother". He transformed his pain into something beautiful. This is what creativity can do: bring healing from hurt, life from loss.

Many people associate creativity with madness. But is this correct? Or merely coincidental? Creative achievements come from both the sound and the unstable. Is it not that creativity is found everywhere, and we remember the most extreme individuals? Or does psychological instability drive a mania and obsession that leads to unreasonable work and breakthroughs? In either case, the stress of a heavy workload must be managed for the longevity and well-being of the creative person.

Between the euphoric moments of discovery there are long black periods where motivation is hard to find. Without emotional resilience, people face a downward spiral. Professor at Yale and creativity researcher Zorana Ivcevic Pringle speaks about creative resilience in terms of emotional regulation. In a conversation with psychologist Scott Barry Kaufman, she spoke of her surprise when she saw how little research there was on creative blocks. Blocks are such a shared and universal experience; they ought to be a well-studied subfield.

A primary focus of Pringle's research is creativity and emotional resilience. Your emotional state is critical to your motivation and creative momentum. Often, when you find yourself creatively stuck, it's worth analysing your emotional states. Have you been stressed? Are you setting too many expectations? Have you been frustrated, sad, anxious? Emotional regulation is key. The creative life can often be lonely—so talk to someone. If you find you are overly stressed and facing burnout—take a break. The prescription is different depending on the problem, but you will develop ways to become more resilient as you embrace your creative potential.

In the next chapters we will talk about putting in place systems of a creative practice. A good practice helps manage the turbulence of creativity and the stress of engaging in challenging environments. Sometimes the work can help you cope and connect with the world. Other times you need to get out of your own way.

CHAPTER 6: PRACTICES

Time – Space – Habits – People

Be regular and orderly in your life so that you may be violent and original in your work.

—Gustave Flaubert

Inspiration is for amateurs, the rest of us show up and get to work.

—Chuck Close

In creative life, consistency is seriously undervalued. To sustain creative work over a meaningful time span, you need more than passion; you need systems and routines. The goal is to align your creative practice with the life you want to live. We can be intentional about making creativity part of our sacred daily rituals with habits that dissolve obstacles and systems that ensure minimal friction. Your process—the elements of your practice—can always improve; you do this by experimenting with the time, space, systems, and collaborators that suit your cycle.

In the MEGA phases, we discussed the "why" and the "what": the motivation behind the work and what kind of work to engage with. In this section we will talk about the "when, where, how, and who" as elements of a creative practice. These are the considerations to ensure your creative engagement is regular and sustainable, optimal and joyful.

First, we look at the "when" of scheduling time each day for the work you want to do. Then we will look at "where"—ensuring that workspaces are optimal. The "how" is the set of habits, triggers, and tactics that can reliably get you working well. And last we talk about the "who"—the people—the kinds of collaborators who lift your level and inspire creativity.

My British South African spelling convention differentiates between *practice* and *practise*. *Practise* is what you do in the Exploration phase—a verb—learning and developing skills for proficiency. The *s* is for sweat. *Practice*, with a *c*—a noun—is the ritual and routines of your creative life. A practice is a constellation of habits, a schedule of creative work. We talk about a practice as a living and breathing thing. Practices are different for every practitioner, and a creative life requires a proliferation of practices.

This chapter documents some of the features of practices that worked for great creative figures. There are no prescriptions, but there are general rules that supercharge sustained creative work and achievement. We can be more scientific about the processes and practices of work without threatening the magic of the work itself. The goal is to direct your energy at the work rather than at *getting* to work.

Optimising elements of practice is not for everyone, but it is the rare individual who would not benefit from at least some of these suggestions. Each of us has an imperfect process that meanders and hums. Your practice is personal. For years I struggled with regularity and focus, so I captured these ideas for myself. Because I procrastinate as much as anyone, I have found it tremendously helpful to keep coming back to the goals of a good practice. And when all else fails, remember this line from Austin Kleon: "Apply ass to chair."

Time (When)

Every morning, without fail, William Faulkner would sit down to write. He began first thing, usually at his home in Rowan Oak, Mississippi. During these hours everything else was subordinated. He wrote until he was mentally exhausted, even stopping mid-sentence at times, and he would not work again until the following morning. His afternoons and evening were sociable and unpredictable, but his morning writing was the consistent and non-negotiable bedrock of his creative life. He committed fully to daily contact with his work. Regardless of place or mood, every day at the same time you would find Faulkner writing.

This section is about routines and how you must consistently schedule time for creative work. This is the "when" of creative work. Your routine is the most impactful thing you can get right; it's arguably the most important part of your creative practice. When you don't have a plan, when you have no idea what to work on, or when you're feeling low—you must still make time to work. Show up and see what happens. Inspiration finds you working.

W. H. Auden said, "Routine, in an intelligent man, is a sign of ambition." Committing to a system and schedule of a daily practice makes creative life more effortless. A regular practice leads to great things because consistency is an underrated superpower. Starting afresh, every day, is the joy and struggle of creative life. Your daily practice is the forcing function that keeps you working. The time you set aside for creative work becomes the blueprint for your process.

Daily Rhythms

In the physiological sciences, researchers talk about a circadian rhythm. We all have an internal clock. This twenty-four-hour biological clock cues us for eating, sleeping, and arousal, and it regulates hormonal release. Circadian rhythm varies person to person, according to our genetic chronotype. This is why some of us are night owls, others are morning larks, and many are fence-sitting birds that can fly either way.

When setting up a sustainable creative routine, it is crucial to understand when you have energy. The question of *when* to work in the day is critical—your schedule must match your circadian clock. The quality of our days is dictated by hormone levels: the intricate release of these chemicals is determined by our light exposure, diet, exercise, as well as genetic code and many other factors. If we are consistent in our days, our hormone levels are more balanced, which can lead to optimal energy and mood. (More on this in the "Health" section.)

There is a time of day, probably different for each of us, when our creative energy flows most fiercely. I thrive in the early morning. After an eight-hour sleep and a strong coffee, I usually have three excellent creative hours. By nine a.m. my energy feels different, depleted, and it's time for admin or exercise or less cognitively demanding work. Each individual must figure out their creative clock and schedule work around their biorhythms. Once you know when you work best, protect your golden hours.

Day Architecture

You can organise your day to optimise for the kinds of engagement you prioritise. Chess prodigy Josh Waitzkin calls this "day architecture." This means scheduling work sessions and life events to match your peak creative energy. Day architecture is about finding the hours of the day that are best for the different parts of your life: work, rest, play, socialising, sleep.

Working every day is far more powerful than long bursts of effort a few times a week because daily habits make a routine, and routine compounds your creative labour. Thirty minutes every day adds up to three hours a week (with a day for rest). Paradoxically, the three hours spread over a week beats a single five-hour session on a Saturday. It is the consistency, the layering of each day's work and ideas, that adds up to great things.

From the research, we know it takes some time to get into a creative frame of mind. The open mode needs time and space to appear, and it needs room to get into a rhythm. It is said that you need something like three hours to get into the flow state. David Foster Wallace said, "I usually go in shifts of three or four hours with either naps or fairly diverting do-something-with-other-people things in the middle."

Author Mason Currey has studied the habits of many great creative figures. In his book, *Daily Rituals: How Artists Work,* he looked at recurring patterns in work structure in figures from Beethoven to Benjamin Franklin. The practices differed wildly. Some, like Flaubert, work late in the darkest hours of night. Others, like Hemingway, prefer the light at dawn.

One feature that stands out in the lives of luminaries is scheduled time for creative work. This is a chunk of time—at least two hours. It is also striking how most of these figures made time for exercise and for socialising in their days. While I would not recommend copying anyone, it is interesting to look at how great creative figures scheduled their days.

You can plan for different phase work at different parts of the day, or alternate phases of work between days. Below is what a MEGA day might look like, twenty-four hours broken up into activity blocks, starting at North when you wake up:

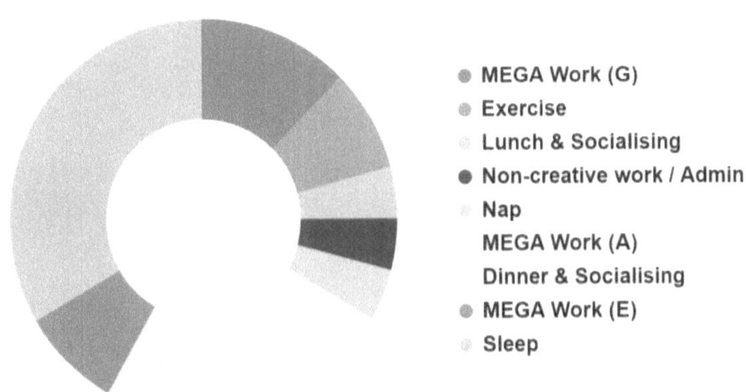

It was David Lynch who said, "The artist's life revolves around working." Set a schedule that you adhere to most days. You might think of breaking your day into different practices—sleep, exercise, meals and socialising, and different sessions for different types of MEGA work. The main idea is that a practice scheduled thoughtfully will feel liberating rather than restricting.

Your routine and mindset must be antifragile to shocks. What happens when life gets in the way? If you truly fall off course, no system will sustain; but you can be adaptable. Use life's caprice as new constraints for your creativity. Update the routine when you must. Reset and reload.

As mentioned before, there are various types of creative work. You may prefer to do your exploration (your vigorous reading and rigorous practising) after dinner and your amelioration (editing work) when you're most awake. You might have a few high-energy hours in the day well suited to generation. You must experiment with the routines of your practice and set aside different parts of the day for different types of creative practices.

Scheduling a starting time is crucial for a reason often cited by habit experts. Most of us experience resistance to starting a task. The more difficult or cognitively demanding the task, the more likely we are to put it off. Scheduling time removes this layer of friction. If we are in the habit of sitting and starting in a systematised way, we give less time for our resisting and procrastinating brains to put things off. Because creativity can be so demanding, it is easy to put off. Scheduling time is one thing, adhering to your schedule is another.

Make time for all the different creative states. Time to wander. Time to practise. Time to polish. Time to analyse. Time to play. Time to collaborate. Time to share. Time to study. Time to move. Time to plan. Time to rest. Time to think. Time to work. Time to create.

Space (Where)

For much of her early research life, Marie Curie worked in a drafty wooden shed behind the School of Physics and Chemistry in the Latin Quarter of Paris—a space so crude it was once used for anatomy dissections, with a leaking roof, warped floor, and air thick with chemical fumes. There, stirring vats of pitchblende for years with an iron rod, she isolated new elements, polonium and radium, and named their strange power "radioactivity."

The shed was an extension of her mind—improvised, solitary, wholly her own—where no institutional lab could restrict her methods. Visitors later called it "a cross between a stable and a potato cellar," and they could not believe that such a place birthed the many discoveries that transformed physics and medicine.

This section is about the "where" of creative work. Author Steven Pressfield said every creative practice needs a physical space. Comedian Larry David's mother always told him, "You have to have some place to go." This is why Maya Angelou rented hotel rooms for her day's writing. Roald Dahl wrote in a dirty shed in the back of his garden in the English countryside. Steve Jobs kept his workrooms fanatically minimalist. As a broke and single mother, J. K. Rowling nursed single cups of coffee for hours in the cafes of Edinburgh.

Physical Memory

In some ways your workspace becomes an extended brain. The space houses physical cues. Like everything in your creative life, the spaces you work in must be tailored to your individual needs. Your spaces for creative work should be accessible, appropriate for your kind of work, and intentionally chosen. You need not have the office garden, or the studio with a view—a clean and uncluttered desk will often do it.

Your space should be conducive to the kind of work you are doing. If you're collaborative, you must be close to co-creators. If focused, you need to find silence. If wildly imaginative, you need to find the place that will provide you with requisite stimulation. Author Donna Tartt wrote her award-winning *The Goldfinch* in the New York Public Library. She would watch the other visitors and use her observations to dress and shape her characters.

Choose the space for the MEGA phase you're in. Noisy communal spaces like a coffee shop or a public park provide stimulus that spark new ideas and perspectives. Quiet rooms are favourites for editing and analytic review. Much of this book was written at a quiet desk overlooking a garden; other parts were written travelling in the frantic bustle of Manhattan; some were written camping in the deep quiet of the Cederberg mountain range. Different places lead to different ways of thinking.

The previous section was about scheduling time; this next section speaks to the engineering of working environment: finding the physical space you require to be creative. As much as creativity loves routine, you also need novelty in your environments. This dance between normalcy and novelty in your practice and environment is a lifelong waltz.

It's best when you have a core space dedicated to creative work. The mind is easily triggered. Our brains are pattern and association machines. When you associate a space with types of creative work, you can pick up more quickly where you left off. We are physical creatures. Spaces house memories. There are myriad cues in an environment that will take you back to an old project or spark an idea learned in the same space. You should have one primary area that anchors all other creative spaces. Treat this area as sacred. Even if this space is temporary, you must protect it from the forces of distraction and procrastination that seek to derail you.

Friction Fraction

Friction is your biggest foe in your creative practice. Friction comes in many forms: procrastination, setting up, cleaning up, phone calls, and all other distractions. How long does it take you from the moment you get to your workstation until you actually get to work? Time yourself. How much time did you have available to work? How much time did you waste? This is your **friction fraction**.

$$\textbf{\textit{Friction Fraction}} = \frac{\textbf{Total time wasted/not working per session}}{\textbf{Total time allocated for creative work}}$$

Your goal is to get this fraction down to a minimum. The waste percentage of your allotted creative time adds up over a lifetime. The smallest hindrance is an excuse for procrastination and faff. Your space should help you reduce friction. The tools you need should be ordered and available. You should not be scrambling to find things, to clear desks, or to make room. Keep your area uncluttered. Keep your devices charged, your pencils sharpened, your materials at the ready. People like to say that "creatives" have messy minds. Well, we're all creative, so then we all have messy minds—you don't need a messy desk as well. The messier you are, the better your systems must be. Creativity must find you ready. Have your draft open. Keep your notebook close. And do not get stuck in the trap of over-optimising.

Mood

Setting up the right environment can be powerful in setting up your mood. Mood is motivation in the moment. Cluttered desks, dirty floors, ugly walls—these influence your mental state. Just tidying up your space ("making your bed" as the self-help gurus proclaim) can have a beneficial impact on attitude and outlook. Tidying up is one of many tips to refresh creativity. This is a physical act (like walking) and resets your creative mood.

There are many elements to a physical space that influence mood. Light, air, colours, noise, decor—these are just some pieces of the environment puzzle. Are the spaces you inhabit full of natural light? Do they have a view of a garden or the sky (however modest)? Do you have plants? Do you play music most conducive to the state of mind you're after? Have you collected decorations that inspire you? Do you have books on the shelf and art on the walls? Is the space well ventilated?

Is your workspace physically comfortable? Get your screen to eye height so you're not straining. Buy the most comfortable chair you can afford. Add a standing desk option. Get a ball you can roll under your feet. Have a yoga mat on hand for stretching during breaks.

Like your routine, optimal settings depend on individual preferences. Every person works differently. You must experiment with your workspace, which is a creative exercise in and of itself. Bring colour and antique uniqueness into your workspaces. Your creative space can reflect the kind of work and personality you aspire to. The better your space, the better your state of mind.

Habits (How)

Beethoven regularly threw buckets of water over his head while composing. Einstein took breaks to nap or play the violin. John D. Rockefeller made lists of his enemies. Every person has a set of systems and habits that help them work. This section gets into the "how" behind creative work. Habits expert James Clear said, "You do not rise to the level of your goals; you fall to the level of your systems." Pair this with David Lynch in *The Art Life,* who said, "You drink coffee, and you smoke cigarettes, and you paint, and that's it."

You will find many contrasting visions on how to work: the anal optimisers, the messy artists, and everything in between. There are many misconceptions about the lifestyles and habits necessary to ignite creativity. There are no silver bullets, but there are guides on what good habits can do for your energy levels and creative output. In this section we speak about organising your tools, living healthily, and proven ways to start your creative session well. As always, do what works for you.

Triggers

How do you kick off a creative session? I think this question is worth obsessing over. The best procrastination beater is to find ways to warm up more quickly. Our brains are not wired to be continually challenged; it's cognitively expensive. We avoid taxing our brains, and any worthwhile creative task is demanding in some way. Triggers provide the quick start or fast warm-up that can trick stress-avoiding brains into working.

Always start small. Do not think about the entire book you want to write. Focus instead on one idea and sentence at a time. Small acts get you into the swing of things. Start a workout with just five push-ups instead of a one-hour schedule (inevitably, a longer workout will follow). Start writing with a single idea or paragraph. Add a few key points for the agenda in a meeting. Never start a session without some small achievable objective to get you going.

Decide what kind of work you're doing. Pick from the MEGA phases. Are you doing research? Do you need to come up with some original ideas? Are you editing your work? Knowing broadly what kind of session is ahead can help you get into the right mental state.

Physical triggers are a whole class on their own. Pair this with the previous discussion of the creative space. Experiment with music and sound and lighting. Music can act as anchor or stimulator for the brain state you want. If you were listening to a certain piece at a point in your project, those sounds can bring you back into the very same creative brain state. Place books or objects around you that remind you of ideas. Put art on your wall that makes you feel certain emotions or ambitions. Dr. Seuss filled his studio with odd hats and strange objects.

Small rituals also make for wonderful triggers. My writing sessions begin with coffee. Caffeine makes my head spin with ideas, and it is my most useful initiator for a creative session. Voltaire famously drank forty cups a day. Find little behaviours that signal to your brain that creative work is starting.

Another type of trigger: shake things up. There are so many ways to freshen each work session. The great musician and producer Brian Eno developed a set of cards for this very reason. The cards are called *Oblique Strategies*. He came up with terms that are designed to change your thought process. He writes out strange little things to get you thinking:

Balance the consistency principle with the inconsistency principle . . .
Trust in the you of now . . .
Emphasise repetitions . . .
You can only make one dot at a time . . .

You can also develop anti-triggers. How do you avoid distraction? How do you leave non-work problems out of the studio? Leave distracting objects at the door. Put up "do not disturb" signs. Set your phone to silent. Best of all, start projects so interesting to you that you can't be distracted. Work truly aligned to your motivation is so effortless it becomes more appealing than mindlessly scrolling media on your phone. Add to your non-distraction tactics. Habits are your tactics: your ready day-to-day behaviours that consistently get you working.

Ernest Hemingway spoke about *leaving something in the tank*. Each session, leave before you have said everything you wanted to. That way you return to your work hungry with unfinished business. Yesterday's work triggers today's. You have an immediate foothold to climb back into a working frame of mind, and an itch that wants to be scratched.

Tools

Each creative domain has a set of tools. Some tools are relevant for all types of creative work. Your evolving understanding of tools is part of your creative evolution. With time a chef understands the importance of a good sharp knife. The guitarist knows a solid wood build gives a richer sound. Getting in touch with your tools is part of the journey of the craft.

With the explosion of technology, there are many new tools available. There are all sorts of technologies that can improve your process. With a certain lens, any useful cultural advances can be seen as new technologies. Ink and scroll, typewriters, computers, chatbots. We continually update how we communicate and thus interact with ideas. The challenge is to match our preferences and proclivities with the tools of the day. How do we use technology for production more than distraction?

Different tools lead you to think and work differently. Videographers will have a favourite type of camera. Some architects prefer hand-drawn to computer-generated plans. New versus old-school is a key decision, you might have to choose between digital and analogue, or you can do both: Clapton plays acoustic and electric. There are many considerations, but we can be more intentional about how our tool use affects the work. Many people become tool collectors rather than tool users. The best tools are those that get you working. It's important to start with those. Once you can identify the tools that serve you best, buy the best ones you can afford. If you can't afford something, be resourceful: build, borrow, beg.

I've fallen into many productivity traps with tools. Not having a certain book becomes an excuse not to write. A dead laptop battery is a reason to watch TV instead. I've wasted hours researching fancy tools I don't need and did not use—time and again I've found the simpler and time-tested fare better.

Whatever the tools at hand, you can always do some kind of work: whether motivational, exploratory, generative, or ameliorative.

Journaling, for example, is a powerful tool that greatly aids the creative mind and process. Regular journaling keeps your thinking organised and your goals clear. A diary or any sort of reflective record can be psychologically repairing and restorative. It's a way to push ideas out of your brain and onto a page. This way your mind feels less chaotic. This very book was a way for me to process, sort, and release all the ideas about creativity I had been collecting.

In *The Artist's Way,* a popular book on the creative life, Julia Cameron recommends something called "Morning Pages." Morning pages is a prescription that asks you to write three pages every morning: hand-written and stream-of-consciousness. It's a form of writing that demands no editing and asks that you keep the pages to yourself. Cameron calls this a "brain drain"—and it's meant for clearing, not creating.

Many of history's most fertile minds were avid journalers. Da Vinci's journals sell for millions at auctions these days; they're the record of a great and curious mind. Journals can hold questions open, they can provide hints as to what you should be working on, and they can capture new ideas as you have them. Journaling is more than the work of note-taking described in chapter 2, "Exploration." Note-taking is explicitly about capturing ideas as you find them. Journal entries let you play with ideas and allow you to be more introspective about your creative process: your failures, your blocks, and your anxieties.

Whatever your preference, writing daily can help you to document progress or simply dump your anxieties and concerns down onto a page. At the very least, it's a container to capture and consolidate good ideas. Some people are very artistic with their journals, making sketches or using beautiful penmanship.

Health

Health and motivation are intrinsically linked. To be in the mood to create, you must have energy. Good health grants this gift of energy, of clear-headedness, and instilling an appetite to be ambitious. The efficient application of creativity depends on many things, but energy is the most important—it is the supercharger of your creative practice. Anything that lifts your energy levels helps the creative process. If you sleep well, you wake up refreshed and energised. If you exercise, your body grows stronger, allowing you to focus for longer. If you eat well, you can be sharp instead of sluggish. If you maintain healthy relationships, you'll have a clearer, more content, state of mind as you chip away at your work.

The basic pillars of physiological health are balanced diet, sound sleep, social connection, sufficient movement, and—I will add—necessary medications. What is necessary and appropriate is for everyone to interrogate and experiment with for themselves. This section is easily condensed; the details of good health are well documented. Habits of wellness require awareness first, then discipline. Once you realise that your health can elevate your work, your experiences, your mood, and all spheres of life, it becomes very costly to eat badly, to stay stationary, to miss sleep, and to avoid people.

Eat well. Move more. Sleep enough. Connect with people. You can make it simple.

Certain healthy habits are common across prolific creative figures. Walking regularly seems like the best kept secret of creative flourishing. A consistent recommendation from our greatest thinkers: take long walks daily. Darwin, Dickens, Tchaikovsky, and Nietzsche are on a list of eager walkers. Walking clears the mind, moves the body, and refreshes the day. Stanford researchers found that walking boosts creative inspiration. They examined creativity levels of people while walking versus sitting. Walking increased creative output by an average of sixty percent. It is to do with the relaxing effect of moving, allowing your mind to marinate ideas in a setting that does not force hard thinking. A long walk—alone, with a friend, in nature, any kind—puts your body and brain in a better position.

It need not always be a walk. Maybe it's a run, or a surf, or yoga—but try to find activities that tick multiple health boxes. Multiple studies now have shown that physical exertion can bolster your creativity. Exercise, at the right intensity, relaxes your mind, allowing creative magic to happen. Daily movement serves your daily routine in several ways. It offers quiet: a period of under-stimulation, a break from the digital storm, and a time to think. A walk offers time in the sun and the shade: natural light in your retina and proximity to green nature. Our monkey bodies need these exposures to thrive.

Haruki Murakami infuses his daily practice of writing with running. His writing is intermingled with his running practice. In What I Talk About When I Talk About Running, *he explains his philosophy of work intertwined with physical movement. Running regulates his mind. Through the daily slog of engaging mind with body, ideas percolating as he pounded the pavement, he has achieved remarkable consistency and beautiful works. Here is an excerpt in his own words:*

"To hold to such repetition for so long—six months to a year [of writing]— requires a good amount of mental and physical strength. In that sense, writing a long novel is like survival training. Physical strength is as necessary as artistic sensitivity."

To close out the discussion on health, we should talk about substances. Most people have complex relationships with substances. It's not something specifically reserved for the most creative people. We confuse stories of great artists who were prolific substance abusers. Inspiration can be found in places other than at the bottom of a bottle or during an acid trip. The Beatles would still have become *The Beatles* without LSD. We might have missed out on "Lucy in the Sky with Diamonds," but how many good Beatles years and songs were we robbed of due to Lennon's heroin habit? Many great artists made great work despite substance intake, not because of it.

Substance abuse substantially diminishes creative life and production. Miles Davis suffered horribly and lost many productive years with his drug use. In the 1980s, Basquiat used substances to sustain brutal painting marathons, and this lifestyle killed him by age twenty-seven. Notably, the number twenty-seven has become significant in the culture because so many young artists self-destructed with substances by this age. The "27 Club" includes Amy Winehouse, Kurt Cobain, Jimi Hendrix, Janis Joplin, and Jim Morrison. For these artists, substances were used to cope rather than to create.

Van Gogh, a problematic absinthe drinker, said this: "Besides, it is a certain fact that I have done better work than before since I stopped drinking, and that is so much gained."

Of course, there are cases where substances induce a shift of consciousness and inspire something—but that is not a recommendation for drugs, it may just as well be a warning. There exists a mismatched bohemian view of the creative lifestyle that threatens good health and sustained creative engagement. This is not to lecture on substance abuse but rather to question how health habits and substances aid creative work. Consume as you must. Each of us has different capacities, demons, needs, tolerances; good health varies by individual. Good health is multifaceted: there are physical, social, and psychological components. The takeaway message is that health can help or hinder our creativity, and you should see these choices as important influences on your creative life and potential.

People (Who)

In the 1970s, the art form of filmmaking was in revolution. A small group called the "Movie Brats" met regularly to discuss the craft. Chief among them were Francis Coppola, George Lucas, Steven Spielberg, and Martin Scorsese. They would spend countless hours breaking down films and plotting their creative futures.

In 1969, Coppola and Lucas founded American Zoetrope. The early encounters between these legendary directors demonstrate the fundamental difference between the two; Lucas was calculated and always strove to make smart business decisions to finance his creative endeavours. Francis, in his own words, "would jump off a mountain without knowing what was down there to land on and that [he] would end up with no money." Coppola and Lucas complemented each other.

The Movie Brats were fiercely competitive and surprisingly collaborative. Their successes would spur each other to greater heights over the next half century. A shared love of the craft united them.

We are social creatures, and creativity is joyful when you find the right collaborators. The "who" of your creative process is critical. You can be more deliberate about the type and regularity of collaboration. You might chase great collaborators or seek a creative milieu. The right people in the right place and time give feedback, energy, and inspiration.

Henry James said it well:

> Every man works better when he has companions working in the same line, and yielding to the stimulus of suggestion, comparison, emulation. Great things have of course been done by solitary workers; but they have usually been done with double the pains they would have cost if they had been produced in more genial circumstances.

Collaboration

It helps enormously to find people who care about creative work, and who inspire you to care also. It's about finding like minds—not necessarily people with the same ideas but rather with a shared creative spirit. They want to make things, be curious with you, and see creativity flourish.

There are too many people out there who will belittle and criticise. Avoid naysayers and critics early on as you work on your motivation and confidence. Your early career and early projects are fragile. Inchoate ideas won't form if they are exposed to the harsh light of criticism too early. Criticism comes later, when your work can withstand it.

Author John Briggs said collaboration is one of the best-kept secrets in creativity. Different levels of collaboration are needed for different MEGA phases in your projects. How you collaborate depends on how you work. Creativity loves company, whether this is in co-creation or seeking an audience. You are not an island. You want to make things people will use or enjoy, and you want to connect with others.

Think about developing a creativity network. This involves finding people who share your love of craft. You can get people together to bounce ideas off, to get feedback from, to go to for support. You are far more likely to sustain if you can find a supportive group. Find just one great collaborator, and your life may change. History is replete with examples of MEGA pairs: Crick and Watson, Lennon and McCartney, the Coen brothers, Simon and Garfunkel, the two Steves (Jobs and Wozniak), Larry Page and Sergey Brin, Marie and Pierre Curie, Laurel and Hardy, Larry David and Jerry Seinfeld, Fry and Laurie; the list goes on.

Collaborators can be a great comfort in every phase. You might meet someone who inspires you—a mentor or a friend. You might want to learn with a group. You might want to generate new ideas with a partner. You may be looking for someone to review your work.

If you invite people into your process at the right time, you may invite magic. Experiment with how you work best and bring people in around your practice. Some people are infectious. Their creative energy fills the room. When you find such people, keep them around. Some people bring great ideas, others bring good vibes and a positive outlook, and others you seek because they have a unique way of seeing the world.

Having the right people around you can make or break creative projects. Negative people will suck the air out of the room. Their criticism will kill promising early ideas. Positive people will accelerate your creative thinking, and they often give you confidence to try things.

We discussed the importance of a feedback mechanism in chapter 4, "Amelioration." Find the right people to give you feedback at the right time. Gather trusted voices around you—they can raise your standards. Friendly folks for the first draft. Harsh critics to attack your final edit.

If you're lucky, you'll find good guides in your creative life. Parents, teachers, mentors—we need creative role models. It really helps to have knowledgeable people to show you the secrets of the world. We are all influenced by those kind enough to share their creative energy. You should remember this and pay it forward when the opportunity arises.

Competition is part of collaboration. One of sport's great warriors, Rafael Nadal, played for the love of the battle. His rivalry with Roger Federer took his game, and the sport of tennis, to new heights. He had to find creative ways to unsettle the mighty Federer forehand.

Competition spurs creativity. Braque and Picasso, Da Vinci and Michelangelo, Coppola and Lucas, Jobs and Gates. The fiercest rivalries changed their domain.

Collectives

Musician and creativity all-rounder Brian Eno is famous for talking about *scenius*: scenes in history that encouraged genius. Medici Florence during the 1500s. Physics in Western Europe in the 1920s. Silicon Valley in the late 1900s. These efflorescent periods in history gave rise to prolific creative production. Creative people gathered to these places and made art and wonderful discoveries.

The very act of being in a certain place, with certain people, at a special time encourages great creativity. Michelangelo laboured to outwork Da Vinci; Heisenberg raced Schrödinger. Monet and Renoir often painted together in the woods of Barbizon, sharing styles and ideas (for a time, it was difficult to distinguish between the work of the two artists).

The world's great cities all have scenius. Writing in NYC feels different than anywhere else; the people give the place undeniable creative energy. Art in Paris feels more profound. Opera in Vienna. Football in Barcelona. Part of it is history and setting, but the most important piece is the people.

Many of us work in organisations. We face "people problems" daily. The collective effort at most companies often feels forced, stilted, drained of creative energy. This often happens when the original founders of the institution have moved on. The creative spirit has left the building—and what's left is procedures and products to maintain. New creative energy is needed in these groups. You can be a source of creative energy where you work by improving things, bringing new ideas, and lifting people up.

In organisations, we often call creativity "innovation." This rarely looks like radical creativity. More often it involves tweaks and improvements to the current process or product. Smaller groups like start-ups are more likely to exhibit strong creativity as the effects of individual creativity become diluted in larger group dynamics.

In 1942, the world was at war. The Allies faced the existential threat that the Nazis could nuclear warheads before they did, which would all but ensure a global fascist order. In America, the great scientists of the West assembled. Funded by the US military and led by the inimitable Robert J. Oppenheimer (and the forceful General Groves), a massive cross-functional team set out to work on perhaps the toughest challenge yet in physics and industrial design (as well as military coordination).

This collaboration has been studied for the better part of a century. Creative problem-solving was needed for every part of the bomb design and industrial development. At Los Alamos, a cadre of world-class physicists and engineers attacked the problem of nuclear theory. Their motivation was clear: protecting the world from evil. Much of the exploratory work had been done over the last few decades. Luminaries like Bohr, Heisenberg, and von Neumann had laid the groundwork for quantum physics. The Manhattan Project physicists had to catapult the current theory into workable designs for atomic warfare. They had to work together to generate a weapon prototype powerful enough to end the war. Three years later, this remarkable group made history.

Our greatest challenges require large creative groups and collaborative efforts. We prefer the image of the lone creative hero, but extraordinary achievements are often the result of well-managed groups, united by shared mission, albeit with a formidable leader. It's a little-known fact that Michelangelo managed thirteen assistants to help him paint the ceiling of the Sistine Chapel. Legendary ad-man David Ogilvy said this about extraordinary groups: "I have observed that no creative organisation, whether it is a research laboratory, a magazine, a Paris kitchen, or an advertising agency, will produce a great body of work unless it is led by a formidable individual."

In his book *Organizing Genius: The Secrets of Creative Collaboration,* Warren Bennis looks at some of the great collaborations of the twentieth century. Disney's first animation group, Lockheed Martin's Skunk Works lab, Xerox and Apple's work on the first computer, Bill Clinton's inaugural electoral campaign, the art and community around the Black Mountain College, and of course, the Manhattan Project. Bennis selected these projects to underscore the range of creative collaboration.

He writes, "Great groups are organisations fully engaged in the thrilling process of discovery." Again, we see this idea of open-endedness and discovery, and what creativity will render when it is not blocked by group dynamics. Creative groups gather around all sorts of goals. Bennis notes that the great achievements united individuals through love of craft or commitment to mission. Sustained creative collaboration requires bonds that are deeper than company contracts. In short, people need good reasons to work together.

Great groups are of course composed of individuals. The seven projects studied were disproportionately composed of young members—people under thirty-five. This balance of youthful energy and experience is delicate. There are moments in history where circumstances necessitated creative collaboration. If scenius was about individuals competing, collaborating, and thriving; collective creation is more about large groups working together with meaningful creative goals.

CHAPTER 7: PROTOCOLS

Constraints – MEGA Switching – Shift Perspective – Keep Momentum

---

Most of us have two lives. The life we live, and the unlived life within us. Between the two stands Resistance.

—Steven Pressfield, *The War of Art*

Author Steven Pressfield has a term for the gamut of anti-creative forces that keep us from doing creative work; he calls it the *Resistance.* The Resistance is everything that keeps us from working and working well. The Resistance employs distraction, demotivation, and destabilising tactics to stop progress. Protocols are the techniques that rage against the Resistance, keeping your creative work whirring and helping you effectively navigate the creative process. Protocols are meta-creative approaches that get you into the right MEGA phase and the right frame of mind. Your creativity cannot be programmed, but it may benefit greatly from good protocols.

Picture your creative process as a road trip down a four-lane highway. Protocols optimise this journey. You start by **framing** your journey with starting constraints: assessing your vehicle, the traffic, the weather, checking your map, and plotting the route. Along the way you need to think about **switching** lanes—choosing the right MEGA phase to progress with. (The stop at the fuel station is a much-needed rest and recharge). At some points you require **shifting** perspective with detours, changing routes, or looking for a 10,000-foot view. Last, and perhaps most important, is to ensure that you keep **moving**.

Setting constraints, alternating phases, changing perspective, and keeping momentum: these are the four classes of protocols we will discuss in this chapter.

FRAME
Choosing the route, the constraints, and where this adventure actually begins.

SWITCH
Choose the right lane for the phase you're in — and refuel when needed.

SHIFT
Rise above the details to see the bigger terrain — new patterns emerge.

MOVE
Momentum is everything. Take the next mile.

Constraints

We're at one of the hottest new jazz spots. The club lights are low. The openers just played their set; the crowd was impressed. Local cats, bright futures. Now for the real show, an international act with a big reputation. Anticipation hangs heavy in the air. As the clock hits the hour, the crowd quiets as they gaze expectantly at the stage.

The trio emerges. A few whoops and some big cheers. The guitarist, the headliner, basks in the applause. He smiles at the crowd and gives a wink. His ponytail whips around as he nods to his drummer and bassist.

"A one, a two, a one two three four..."

He starts with tempo. Edgy notes from the start. Some funky shit. A few in the crowd are nodding their heads intensely to the beat, eyes closed, trying to work out the moves.

A few minutes in, people start muttering. The guitarist is still going rogue, and there's no discernible melody yet. Some of the more serious jazz fans smirk and quiet the audience—he is playing "way outside," they say. This is "really excellent." A few more minutes pass, and even the die-hards stop smiling. Single notes are still coming in irregular intervals, out of tempo. The ponytail continues to bob out of beat. The drummer gives up; the bassist seems to be playing by himself. There is no key and no chords—there's absolutely zero structure. A truculent fellow in a beret starts booing at the back, and the rest of the crowd join in, until the musicians cannot be heard. Someone throws a bread roll at them, and the trio scarper off the stage. The show is over.

Creativity without constraints is chaos. You cannot make sense of endless options without guides, limits, and rules. In other words, one must first fix the frame to begin the work. A domain requires a set of rules and internal organisation. You can break the rules later, but you need to operate according to some ordering principles.

One definition of anxiety is *the inability to choose among too many options.* Following constraints gives you a foothold in each of the MEGA phases. You work according to your practical limitations: your interests, talents, values, and time available. Even your past experiences form personal constraints in which your agency and identity is rooted. Orson Welles said, "Limitations breed creativity." At each phase, welcome constraints. Later, you can lift them or choose new ones—but constraints tether your creativity so that it can be usefully and specifically applied. Jerry Seinfeld said, "The brain is so easy to master, you just have to confine it."

In this chapter, we'll look at three kinds of constraints. First, the constraints of initial conditions. At the start of every project you have constraints of self and circumstance: what you know, what you can do, and the tools at hand. Then we'll look at constraints of craft: These are the rules of your chosen domain. Last, we'll talk about the ultimate constraint of time, and why setting deadlines can unleash great work.

Starting Conditions

The key to kicking off your creative process is working with what you have. Every constraint helps to focus and direct creative energy on what is possible right now. Creativity loves constraints. This idea may not be new to you, but you might have underestimated the role of constraints in creative work. The domain you operate in, the tools available, the ideas floating in your mind, the time and environment allocated to work, your style, your voice, and your experiences are all constraints. All these things happily narrow the possibilities of your creative engagement and the scope of work at hand.

The highly productive among us do not make excuses; they work within the current limitations and simply treat obstacles as constraints. There are so many ways to think about constraints and to reframe any limitation as a new guide for creative work.

The best story I could find about working with constraints is Keith Jarrett's legendary performance in Cologne:

It was a miserable January night, an hour before the concert. The rain lashed down, and a biting cold surrounded the Köln opera house. Still, there was energy and anticipation—the show was sold out. Pianist virtuoso Keith Jarrett had just arrived in town. By this time, in 1975, Jarrett was a sensation in the jazz world, having recently played with greats like Miles Davis, Art Blakey, and Charles Mingus.

But on this particular night, Jarrett was tired and hungry. He had just made a long drive across Europe after transferring his plane ticket for cash to drive with a producer friend. His supper at a nearby restaurant had also been cut short as they needed to get to the venue. Jarrett started warming up on the piano, but he soon stopped and waved over the show's organiser. He could not play on this instrument. It was out of tune, the keys on the upper and lower register did not respond well, and the pedals were broken. Jarrett refused to play the concert.

This was a nightmare scenario for organiser Vera Brandes. At eighteen years old, she was one of the youngest promoters in history, and Jarrett had been a major get. In the preceding hours, a catastrophe had unfolded. The opera staff had been told to bring the concert grand Bösendorfer 290 Imperial, but somehow they had found a smaller baby grand Bösendorfer backstage that was for rehearsals only, and it was in a bad state.

Due to the rain and the late hour, there was no question of bringing in another instrument. This was it, broken baby Bösendorfer or the show called off. In one of the great feats of persuasion, Brandes cajoled Jarrett into playing. The recording equipment had already been set up, and it would be very expensive to cancel for all parties. A cantankerous Jarrett—already a moody fellow in the lightest of times—sat back down at the battered piano and readied himself for the show.

What happened next went down as one of the great performances in jazz history. The Köln recordings would become both the best-selling piano and solo album in jazz, selling four million copies. The piano was unplayable by any reasonable standard. But as soon as he decided he would play the show, Jarrett lost himself in the challenge. While playing, he mapped the areas of the instrument that would give him any sort of sound, and he listened intently to his audience, improvising and adapting to the limited influence and the energy of the crowd. He stuck to the middle part of the keyboard and used a rolling technique to get a deeper bass sound from the tinny keys. Using a mesmeric style of vamping over chords for long stretches, Jarrett varied his style between slow rubato and a bluesy gospel feel.

No one could have scripted the music that came out of Jarrett that night, not even Jarrett himself. The beat-up piano, the mesmerised crowd, the cold weather in West Germany, his tired state—on this fateful night these conditions led him somewhere special.

Form

Constraints appear at every phase of the creative process. The need for constraints is most evident when faced with the blank canvas or an empty page. In the Discovery Space, constraints are the light cone for your output. You cannot produce something beyond your abilities, just as you cannot travel faster than the speed of light. You traverse creative domains according to constraints. Current ideas and obstacles rise up as your stepping stones. Your chosen style and the ceiling of your knowledge limit your creative paths. Ignorance is a powerful constraint—it's easy to break rules you haven't learned yet.

Anything can act as a constraint. The choice you made to operate in this domain is a constraint. Choose a style. Choose a method. Choose *something*. Constrain yourself to find a foothold in the infinite possibility of your creative pursuit. And then loosen the constraints. Tighten and then loosen. This is the heaving and breathing art of creativity.

All domains are arbitrary in some way, but we fix domains so that we can crystallise certain dimensions of life in each moment—to make sense of things and to advance our knowledge or understanding in some way. This is true for any creative domain, be it art, science, or business.

Creativity has a love–hate relationship with rules and structure. To start, everyone must learn the structure to operate in a domain. These rules give welcome initial constraints: rules make forms. Form illuminates the structure from which creativity springs. Jazz musicians welcome the form of standards. Shakespeare's use of iambic pentameter unlocked some of the finest writing in the English language. The convention of the academic paper forces rigour into our collective truth-seeking.

It is critical to learn how to work with the rules of the domain and to stay within the borders of the art form; to play within the box until you find original ideas to break out of it.

This advice always sounds counterintuitive in the freewheeling world of creative engagement, but it is one of the most important messages of this book: *embrace constraints*. Advertising executive Stephen Hall has a memorable saying about creativity without constraints: it's like trying to play squash without walls—it just doesn't work. A Borges Space cannot be navigated without constraints. To operate in a vast sea of choice, you must pick one action at a time. So, you narrow your gaze, fixing on one piece of the horizon to aim at, making progress, then lifting your sights again.

Somewhere in your creative growth, you will develop a style. Some people call this your "voice." This is yet another welcome constraint. But constraints must be wielded carefully. Hold them lightly so that you are not kept stuck in your creative past. You can expand your style with time, and your constraints will change accordingly.

Our creative voice can be seen as a dynamic and welcome constraint. Our interests limit the Borges Space we play in. In these spaces, our curiosity limits what we explore. Our knowledge and ideas limit what we generate. Our tastes limit the final piece of work that we converge upon. Your view of the world is utterly unique, and so are your constraints.

There are many introductory exercises to help you think about constraints as aids in creative work. My guitar teacher once suggested the following exercise: Use just one string of the guitar and come up with a tune. Make a melody one note at a time. With this constraint, I started to see the role of spacing notes, the dynamic possibilities when picking louder or softer, and the possibilities offered by repetition and pause. Constraining your choices even in obvious ways can lead to deeper understanding. Creativity lecturer James C. Kaufman gets his students to write short essays without using the letter *e*. Dr. Seuss only allowed himself fifty words in *Green Eggs and Ham*.

The most generative people in the world actively cultivate constraints. They constrain themselves to one field and project at a time, and see what they can do with what they have, and then absorb themselves in the new possibilities. Without constraints you face the crippling anxiety of infinite choice. No decision can be made in the face of this overwhelming array of options. You need lines in the sand to start.

Parkinson's Law

Author Adriana Trigiani said, "There's nothing an artist needs more—even more than excellent tools and stamina—than a deadline." Now seems like a good time to tell you about Parkinson's law, the constraint of time.

Part of the challenge in the amelioration process is finding the discipline to finish your projects. Creativity has many great foes: apathy, conformity, procrastination. Apathy is deadly. Conformity is crippling. Procrastination is complicated. We are capable of so much, but our distractible and fragile attention requires guidance. We've mentioned practices, we've looked at protocols, now we will discuss production deadlines.

In 2015, the NYC filmmaker Casey Neistat started posting daily video blogs (vlogs) on YouTube. He did this every day for more than two years, without missing a day. That's over 800 days: 800 stories, 800 late nights of editing, 800 videos for his YouTube channel. He filmed constantly and the editing work stacked up to hundreds and thousands of hours. Incredible things started to happen. Millions subscribed. People from all over the world followed his films and adventures. His editing skills rose to the level of artistry, and he became a YouTube sensation. His technology business took off, his marriage almost ended, and major sponsors offered million-dollar ad deals.

The critical decision was to adhere to a prolific production schedule. His daily deadline catapulted Casey to extreme creative engagement—great videos, stardom, and opportunity followed. But it was the decision to create each and every day that is so interesting. Neistat decided to be prolific, and the world loved it. Of course, the unreasonable deadlines meant he burnt out badly and faced family problems. There were days where he could not conceive of creating another script, another edit, another video—but for 800 days and more, he persisted. It was in this wild period that he forged and found new dimensions in his creative process. He was pushing so hard that he simply had to find new arrows in his quiver. This is what extreme deadline-driven momentum can do: skills compound; opportunities appear.

Neistat was in his thirties when he did this. Now he lives at a more leisurely creative pace, but that intense time made him. What is the equivalent constraint in your creative world? What can you do that lifts you out of the humdrum of low expectations, that takes you way out of your comfort zone? How can you achieve the work of decades in years, or of years in weeks?

In 1955, C. Northcote Parkinson—a British naval historian—wrote an essay based on his observations about administration, management, and bureaucracy in the navy. His critical insight, one that he would later turn into a book, endures to this day—it's now called *Parkinson's law*. This idea is: "Work expands so as to fill the time available for its completion." In other words, the demands we make of ourselves limit or expand our potential. Ambitions and goal-setting matter.

Parkinson's law is an inspiration to get a little more out of the day by setting more ambitious deadlines. This is not to adhere to harebrained prescriptions for productivity, but rather to aim our limited time and energy at the things that matter.

There are challenges associated with deadlines. Generous deadlines lead to procrastination, but overly rigid deadlines dampen exploration. The trick is to recast deadlines as liberator rather than detractor to your work. Deadlines can be used to refocus and to help prioritise the most important creative work. This is how you ensure deadlines do not kill the open mode. You can wield Parkinson's law to become prolific.

The very term *deadline* contains a morbid reminder that life is finite. We all have an ultimate deadline—quite literally, there is a bright finish line ahead for us all. In his book *Four Thousand Weeks: Time Management for Mortals*, Oliver Burkeman reminds us exactly how much time we have. Instead of viewing our finitude as cosmically negative, Burkeman encourages us to view life's glass as half full: We all have pages left to write. There is always time left: counted in days, months, or decades. The heavy fact that our weeks are numbered invites an urgency to choose creative work that matters—and to get going.

MEGA Switching

Momentum falters, focus fades, interest wanes. How you manage creative blocks will define your creative life. Blocks are always looming, and they vary in type and severity. They have many forms: burnout, misalignment, apathy, feelings of inferiority, procrastination, lack of inspiration, self-doubt, debilitating uncertainty, feeling stuck. Every project offers some new cocktail of blocks: avoidance blocks, distraction blocks, inertia blocks. There are more varieties of blocks than there are creative people. Switching protocols are designed to beat these blocks. Most blocks can be beaten by switching to the right phase of creative work at the right time. Focusing on the right MEGA phase at the right moment is the most effective way to beat blocks.

Many fall prey to favouring a single phase. The lifelong learner is always exploring, never generating. The generative artist is always full of ideas, never practising their craft or polishing their work. The eager editor is stuck refining the same project, unable to move on and share their work. We have established the different creative phases; now we can think about navigating between these phases.

Few creative projects will progress smoothly from M to E to G to A. In fact, almost no project will progress like this. You will start in unexpected places, and you will mostly switch between phases unconsciously. When you become stuck in one place, you can think about these switching protocols. The switch you need depends on where you are in your project and the nature of your problem.

Work happens in bursts, and insights strike in strange order. Creativity researcher Keith Sawyer calls it the *zig-zag path*; he says, "A truly successful creative process is wandering, exploratory, and iterative." You may need to zig to the Exploration phase or zag to amelioration. Your issue could be that you've selected the wrong problem and you must return to the Motivation phase.

In this section we'll talk about timely protocols for switching into and out of phases. We also introduce the powerful and forgotten phase of rest. The transitions described in this section are the most common pitfalls when navigating between the different phases.

The First Switch

Putting Motivation to work: *Following your problem into the other phases.*

The first switch is about putting motivation to work. Motivation is not a phase to linger in. Once you have an inkling of the work that attracts you, you must move quickly to a different phase to test whether your interest truly lies in this field. Try painting. Write a short story. Buy the best textbook on the topic. The trick to a rich creative life is getting good at starting things.

Too many people never try. Having a bias for action eliminates the ponderous inactivity that most people experience. More is learned through failure than through success. You cannot wait until you're sure that a field is for you—try things quickly and learn. Think of these immortal words by Samuel Beckett, "Ever tried. Ever failed. No matter. Try again. Fail again. Fail better."

Author David Epstein said, "We learn who we are in practice, not in theory." The process of motivation is never-ending. Most people, even the most successful, will reinvent themselves and discover new motivation many times in their lives. This is part of the creative condition.

Crossing the In-Between

Exploration to Generation: *From Learning to Breaking the Rules, Search to Discovery, Old Map to New Map, Dot Collector to Dot Connector, Breathing In to Breathing Out, Reader to Writer*

Because exploration is partly passive, it's very easy to stay in this mode indefinitely. We're satisfying our curiosity but, if we stay here without progressing, we're denying an innate call to create. Our brains bubble with new ideas; they cannot stop generating. The problem is that we've learned to repress these new ideas. We refuse ourselves licence because we've decided "we're not creative." Many people think that their creative potential ends around the exploration phase. The zone between exploration and generation is fraught with traps. I call it the *In-Between*. It's a bit like purgatory; some will never leave.

The steps before generative creativity invite the most misgivings to creep in. To allow creativity to be realised, you need to ignore your doubts and cross the void. The switch to generation needs no ceremony. It can be as simple as turning away from reading a book to writing down an idea. So many of us resist this powerful impulse to generate. We stay fixed in the Exploration phase and deny our urgent creative instincts. We become so used to learning rather than creating that a passive paralysis sets in. Consumption is comforting—we feel like we're making progress. But by failing to strike when new information is hot, we miss an opportunity to generate something new.

The In-Between zone is hard to traverse without experience. We fear the next phase in which we must attempt to say something new, where failure is likely. And we're desperately afraid we won't be any good. We're intimidated by the great works and masters; we throw our hands up and say, "I can never do that." Well, you probably can't. But you *can* do something different and great in your own way—but only if you learn to switch to the Generation phase more often. To fully enter the Generation phase, you must break the imaginary shackles on your potential, on your self-styled identity.

The switch from exploring to generating is the greatest mindset change in creative work. It requires you change from consumer to producer, explorer to creator, the known to the unknown, search to discovery. Maybe it comes back to courage. It takes real courage to put your neck on the line and shoot for originality. But these are the important questions to remember when you feel scared: Who do you want to be? What kind of things do you want to see in the world? What can you make that's your own?

I can share more concrete advice to become generative from the legendary British comedian John Cleese, who is a great student of the creative process. Supported by research of Donald MacKinnon from Berkeley University, Cleese talks about the *open mode* (introduced in chapter 3, "Generation"). To break out of the Exploration phase and to get into a generative mode, Cleese recommends five steps. In a talk to London society, he outlined them: *Space, Schedule, Time, Confidence, and Humour.*

- **Space**: Create room away from your usual humdrum existence, where you aren't under pressure, where there isn't the usual noise of your life. Find an environment that invites freedom for exploration and playful divergent thinking.
- **Schedule**: Set aside time for creativity. Put it in your schedule as nonnegotiable, blocked-out time. All your best ideas and greatest insights will flow from these blocks of creativity.
- **Time**: Creativity can be summoned, but it can take a while. Sometimes you need to settle into the flow slowly, and you can't press too hard. Research shows that you might need as long as three hours to get into the swing of the open mode and into the generative state of mind. Allow extended periods of time without pressing too hard for output.
- **Confidence**: Don't be afraid of making a mistake. Don't be afraid of looking foolish. Creativity requires confidence and courage. Be yourself with confidence and watch how creativity flows.
- **Humour.** Of course, a professional comedian would add this last point, but it's true that humour invites a certain irreverence and relaxing of rules. Laughter is a wonderful way to put you in a certain mood and grant the kind of lightness and openness required to generate.

These recommendations match up partly to the sections of the practice chapter. Good practices allow you the space and time to notice new ideas as they arrive.

It is not always the transition from exploration into generation that's the problem, sometimes it's the reverse. Many will start their creative project with original ideas. But these kinds of artists and undisciplined enthusiasts struggle with switching out of generation. New ideas are not the problem, rather they avoid the hard work of exploration which requires practising and rigorous learning. An example of someone unable to switch back to exploration is a scientist who writes papers without fully understanding the literature. Another is a musician who composes songs of poor quality because they haven't shored up their understanding of theory, chord variation, or song structure. Another is an artist who doesn't develop technique and can therefore never realise the ambition of their imagination.

Some talented few have an innate ability to move straight to creative breakthroughs, but most of us need to do the hard work of exploration first. If you are generative and struggling with the quality of your production, a switch back to exploration is required to build skills and fetch new ideas that can be brought back into future generation phases.

Hot to Cold

Generation to Amelioration: *Open to Closed, Divergent to Convergent, Ideation to Execution. Writer to Editor*

Generation requires open-mode, hot, divergent creativity. The next mode of creative work is the closed, cold, convergence of Amelioration. The Amelioration phase calls for critical assessment of what you've produced. Where generation was intuitive, amelioration is analytical. Switching between creation and criticism requires switching between non-judgemental and judgemental approaches. This is difficult to do in the same session, so it's best to find some breathing room before you switch.

Amelioration work is dangerous too early or when new ideas are fragile. You cannot bring in criticism too early as you may quell promising nascent ideas. But wait too long and you can struggle with direction. The switch to amelioration is all about timing: You want to wait until you have generated enough to edit meaningfully and then begin the review of your work to see where you are coming up short.

Generation and Amelioration are the phases of active creation. You are building and shaping your work. There are two distinctly different states of mind required for each of these phases. Switching between the two is an art that is improved with experience.

If you spend too long in either, your pile of new ideas becomes too daunting to sift through; or you become inured to work not sufficiently alive with originality. Alternating timeously between generation and amelioration is critical; it's like jumping between the sauna and the ice bath without overheating or freezing.

Rest

The Neglected Phase: *Rest is the punctuation in the long book of your creative life.*

Drive three hours from Cape Town along the West Coast of South Africa, from the cold white spray of the Atlantic through vast tracts of farmland, and you will hit upon a famous mountain range called the Cederberg. For three hundred kilometres, these mountains impose themselves on the landscape. They invite you from a long way out.

As you ascend into the peaks you lose all forms of reception, landmarks disappear, the road degrades into rough gravel. Your view becomes consumed by the Fynbos vegetation in bits of colour—yellow, green, and brown. Blue sky and mountain greens. If you go up the pass, to the river on the top, the grassy glades await. There is quiet here. Parts of this book were written in these mountains. Often when you come to a place to rest, ideas flow like soft streams after summer rain.

Rest is essential in your creative life. It is the forgotten phase of creativity, but the pauses are an important part of your MEGA process. You need space and time for your ideas to breathe. Rest is a between state not mentioned explicitly before. It allows you to let things simmer and return to the work with energy and ideas. There is wisdom in the weekend. Rest is the remedy for burnout. Good rest charges good work.

Rest should not be a once-a-year-on-the-holidays occurrence. Strategic breaks are required regularly. It is important to rest both in between sessions and in between projects. The road to burnout is paved by half-finished works, or over-ambitious deadlines. You need to find the right pacing. Sometimes you need to get away from the daily hustle to let the work breathe, to let your brain settle itself, and to return refreshed and revitalised. By taking a break, or leaving the draft in your desk drawer, you can switch from author to editor to learner (and vice versa) and assess your work more clearly.

In his lovely book, *Rest: Why You Get More Done When You Work Less,* Alex Soojung-Kim Pang elevates rest as an essential creative protocol. Pang talks about his four big insights on rest as part of a creative and productive life. First, he says, work and rest are partners: our brains keep working in states of rest, and inducing states of rest within our creative practice lets our unconscious processes solve problems. Second, rest is active: it's not just naps and passivity and inactivity; rest can be gained through exercise, walks, and physical challenge—in fact, many of the levers of good health are also levers for rest. Rest for the mind can be gained by exertion in the body, as stronger bodies result in minds that are clearer and sharper. Third, Pang writes, rest is a skill: Rest must form part of your practice; you must find the kinds of rest that work for you and get better at harnessing the power of good rest. Finally, the fourth of Pang's insights is that deliberate rest stimulates and sustains creativity. He argues that rest is not merely a means of recovery; it can also be used as a tool to enhance your work and process. Rest in the right amounts each day sharpens and energises and inspires.

Oliver Sacks, in his wonderful essay "The Creative Self," writes,

> Creativity involves not only years of conscious preparation and training but unconscious preparation as well. This incubation period is essential to allow the subconscious

assimilation of one's influences and sources, to reorganise
and synthesise them into something of one's own.

In the Wallas four-stage model of creativity, creativity researchers reference preparation, incubation, illumination, and verification. The MEGA phases map well to these stages, but the incubation state occurs not once but between the explicit phases of work.

When you rest between work, you let good ideas consolidate. Most people understand the benefits of sleeping after studying. This period of rest immediately after learning or creative engagement has mysterious benefits for your problem-solving. You wake up having made progress. Our deep brain states keep at problems even when you stop actively working on them.

Incubation lets your unconscious mind do the work. Rest and reducing workload allow us to take advantage of our unconscious creative capacities. For a plant to thrive and flower, you give it the right soil and enough water and some sunlight—and then you leave it to grow.

Each phase of MEGA work benefits from time away.

One great indicator of whether you are resting enough is boredom. You should feel bored from time to time. The problem with modern life is we are constantly stimulated. We think we are resting when we are scrolling newsfeeds or watching TV, but this is not rest: it is passive, but it is still consumption. Our minds are not being allowed to savour and connect the good ideas, as they are lost in a sea of stimulation. Boredom is how we beat back the tidal wave of information threatening to drown us.

This is why people get into nature, or take walks, or leave their phones in another room—so that we can force quiet into our busy days. When our minds are not engaged, they wander. When our minds are allowed more space, they tend to be more creative. Boredom is a time-tested technique to invite creative ideas. Because our minds are never still, when we stop bombarding them, creativity comes.

Many creative thinkers extol the virtues of monotonous tasks: they let the mind wander. Jeff Bezos claims he still washes his own dishes (yeah, right!). David Lynch worked a tedious printing job in Philadelphia: in these long hours he conceived of his first film, *Eraserhead.* In the early 1930s, J. R. R.

Tolkien was grading a large stack of student exams at Oxford; as he tired of marking scripts, he scribbled in the margin of one paper: "In a hole in the ground there lived a hobbit."

Alternating Projects

The Juggling Act: *Switching Between Domains or Projects.*

MEGA switching is primarily about alternating between phases of work when working on a project. But how should you think about switching between projects? This is a question I struggle with often. There is a cost to switching between domains or projects: you lose momentum (more on this later). For generalists like me, it is very difficult to keep to one project at a time. I think many struggle with an intellectual or creative attention deficit. I like writing, I like playing music, I like reading history. But I've found that multitasking and constant project-switching creates a lot of friction and frustration. It takes me too long to get back into the particular groove of a new project or domain. My working memory is not full of the ideas I need to readily recall. It seems like the best course for me is to pick one major project where I feel I can do great work. For the past few years, it has been writing this book.

Some people enjoy this project- and domain-switching, and if you are producing things and feel engaged, then that's wonderful. But if you're like me and struggle with scattered interests, try to pick one primary project at a time to connect meaningfully. Revisit your motivation and ask honestly where your attention wants to go. And this does not mean you can't keep playing on the side!

Shift Perspective

Salvador Dali said, "Knowing how to look is a way of inventing." The ability to be creative relies on getting into the right frame of mind. We need to find reliable ways to inject novelty into our process and shift our perspective. The focus of MEGA switching was interphase change, but this section focuses on *intraphase* change—finding new angles and approaches applicable within each MEGA phase. The shifting protocols we will talk about entail 1) novelty-seeking and 2) different modes of thinking.

Injecting Novelty

It has been said that no surprise for the writer means no surprise for the reader. You have to find ways to surprise yourself in your work. Each of the MEGA phases calls for this novelty—breaking out of existing patterns to find a different structure of thinking and original perspective. There are techniques to do this more reliably.

Life is a dance between normalcy and novelty. Invite too much novelty, and your process becomes unstable; too little, and your approach atrophies. You will need to develop ways to break your default modes and administer novelty in careful doses.

The easiest way to find novelty is by going somewhere new. Simply transport yourself, and your creative brain must follow. Changing your environment is one tried-and-tested method to change perspective. This could mean working from a different station for a day, like a coffee shop or mountaintop. Or it could mean travelling to a different country and letting the foreign culture refresh your outlook. It also includes new intellectual terrain—learning about a field or subject that is foreign to you. Carl Sagan once expressed an idea that reading is a kind of time travel: that you are climbing into the mind of someone at a different place at a different time. If you can't afford to travel, travel to the library.

Injecting novelty into the creative process can be a deliberate act. You can make this part of your practice. For example, in the first or last few minutes of a session, you can make it a habit to read a page from a random book. Or every third session you must work from a new environment.

You can plan ways to sustain originality: you can use structured or semi-structured approaches designed to break patterns, bypass habits, and provoke surprise. These protocols act like controlled disruptions to the familiar. Here are five practical ideas to inject novelty in your process:

---

1. Arbitrary Constraints

How it works: Flip the constraints of the problem or impose arbitrary new ones.

Example: A songwriter bans all use of major chords. A painter uses only two colours. A writer forces each paragraph to start with a question.

Purpose: This limits the familiar pathways and directs towards surprising or neglected regions of Possibility Space.

---

2. Swap Domains

How it works: Import methods, metaphors, or patterns from unrelated fields.

Example: A software designer studies the form of jazz improvisation.

Purpose: Novelty often comes from cross-pollination—offering new configurations discovered by applying the rules of a different domain.

---

3. Shake It Up

How it works: Use random words, images, sounds, or data to spark associations.

Example: A writer flips open a dictionary and uses the next word as a prompt.

Purpose: Randomness is a tool for circumventing the default pathways of the mind.

---

4. Break It Up

How it works: Break an existing work (yours or someone else's) into parts, then remix them in a new order or format.

Example: A teacher writes out their lesson as a comic strip. A filmmaker edits their movie backwards.

Purpose: This dislodges assumed structures and surfaces unnoticed possibilities.

---

5. Set a Timer

How it works: Restrict or structure time to amplify urgency and disrupt overthinking.

Example: Ten ideas in ten minutes. One sketch every hour for a day.

Purpose: Compression of time forces instinctive, raw, unfiltered creativity.

Creative States of Mind

Certain states of mind refresh your creative process. Creativity calls for different approaches at different times in your life and projects. Just as you switch between the creative phases, you also need to switch between mental models.

This section looks briefly at some modes helpful for shifting or refreshing your creative state of mind: play, humour, and adventure. There are many others, of course, but the following are good examples of altering your approach:

1. Play

Playfulness is more than protocol; it is an essential attitude in creative work. When you find work that feels like play, everything becomes easy. People forget that work can be fun, and that it should be! We are so serious about achievement, about genius, about outcomes. As children, our imaginations compensated for lack of life experience. Play is automatic when we are young. Then life teaches us with bad schools and hard knocks that we must have goals and objectives, and we lose this sense of play. These pressures narrow our vision and kill our sense of fun. But it is this ability to play, to laugh, that unlocks our creativity.

There is a lightness in play. The sections in chapter 1, "Motivation," highlighted our childhood intrigues as hints to our creative passions. As children, we could not help but follow the fun. Play forms part of protocols because play is relevant in all MEGA phases. In the Exploration phase, this will manifest in wanting new things to learn. In the Generation phase, a playful spirit keeps us seeking original ideas.

Philosopher David Deutsch advocates something called the *fun criterion*. This states that people enjoy open-ended and creative work and are exhausted by the repetitive and simple. Play keeps searching for surprises. We find good problems by following our sense of play and fun. The key point is that we do not fully know ourselves. Some of our knowledge is conscious, but a lot of it is unconscious. Fun is the best guide; it is a feeling that will consider many of our inaccessible ideas and preferences. Play surfaces these hidden aspects.

2. Humour

Some things are innate in humans. These features can heighten our creative experience, and one such feature is our sense of humour. Newborns smile and laugh long before they learn to communicate verbally. Humour is a great ally to creativity because it helps you change your approach. Finding something funny can loosen your whole perspective. Most crucially, humour puts people in the open mode.

Arthur Koestler, in his book *The Act of Creation*, stresses humour as an essential manifestation of creativity. Koestler thinks of the Generation phase as bringing together unrelated structures of thinking: a feat he calls *bisociation*. He lists humour as the most immediate example. When you joke, you set the premise, but the punchline always surprises. At its best, humour is a high-wire act of timing, context, and surprise—requiring the same sensitivity to nuance, rhythm, and human nature as poetry or music. Great comedians, like great artists, are pattern-breakers and meaning-makers—holding up a mirror to reality but tilting it just enough to show the absurdity we'd otherwise miss.

Play is closely linked to humour—just watch kids laugh as they play. And humour allows us to loosen our grip on things. We become sillier, more relaxed, and more receptive to the endless new ideas and observations swirling around us. Humour suspends the rules. There is a sense in humour.

3. Adventure

In August 1914, Ernest Shackleton set out on the Imperial Trans-Antarctic Expedition aboard the Endurance, *aiming to make the first land crossing of the Antarctic continent. In January 1915, the ship became trapped in pack ice in the Weddell Sea and drifted northward for months before being crushed and sunk in November. Shackleton and his twenty-seven-man crew camped on the ice until April 1916, when they launched lifeboats and reached the uninhabited Elephant Island. From there, Shackleton and five others sailed over 1,300 kilometres in the twenty-two-foot lifeboat* James Caird *through the treacherous Southern Ocean to South Georgia Island. After landing on the wrong side of the island, Shackleton and two crew members hiked across its mountainous interior for thirty-six hours to reach a whaling station. He then organised multiple rescue attempts, finally returning to Elephant Island in August 1916 to rescue the remaining men. All twenty-eight crew members survived the ordeal.*

At some points in your creative life, you need to take risks. Entrepreneurs say the biggest risk you face is not taking enough risks. A creative mind cannot stay in the same place or keep doing the same thing. You must launch new ventures, travel to foreign lands, and find new dragons to slay. Adventure accelerates your journey to the frontiers of Possibility Space.

Adventure begins where certainty ends—when plans dissolve and where intuition, improvisation, and adaptability must take over. In unfamiliar terrain, the adventurer becomes a problem-solver, constantly translating surprise into strategy, setback into story. Creativity thrives in this state of heightened attention, where the stakes are real and the outcomes are unknowable. Adventure requires you to adopt new ways of thinking and break preconceived models of the world. This also encourages boldness, courage, and other fire-starter qualities that your creative process may need.

Your creative life is the sum of your creative decisions and actions. Intentions don't count that much. It's what you do that will define you. You face a series of choices but keep one warning in mind as you progress: *don't play it too safe*. Remember the graph of flow in chapter 1, "Motivation": one axis is your skill level, and the other is the challenge of the task. You must keep challenging yourself by lifting the bar. Stagnation is creative death; you must seek out projects that daunt you, and end projects when they run their course. When making great art, seeking new scientific mysteries, or testing new ideas in business or engineering, it's essential that you don't keep producing the same old thing. You must take calculated risks.

In chapter 1, "Motivation," we spoke about all the consequences of problem selection. All problems are not equal. You can choose to solve problems that change the world, that help people, that inspire people, that meaningfully impact society. When you are faced with easy problems versus hard and worthy problems, consider the road with greater adventure. You'll learn more, and you'll live more—even if you fail. Worthy problems make you feel out of your depth, out at sea, unmoored—completely caught up with the tide. It is by tackling these weighty and worthy problems that you find anchors for your creative work.

Keep Momentum

With around sixty-five titles, Stephen King writes a book a year. He says momentum matters more than brilliance. Woody Allen has produced a film a year for almost fifty years. He said it was about continuity more than perfection. Prince released thirty-nine studio albums. Bach, driven by the church calendar, produced a new cantata nearly every week.

Most impressive was Picasso. Over his lifetime, across eight decades, Picasso produced close to 150,000 works. Thousands upon thousands of paintings, prints, illustrations, and sculptures. If you calculate the daily rate of production, that's over five pieces a day. Picasso was promiscuous in his projects and output. Every day he would get up and create new works. His early stuff was accused of being highly derivative. Some sketches were uninspired. Some of his ideas did not work out. But he kept producing; through rain and shine, success and failure, he kept going.

Producing work is easier when the wind is behind your back. The most prodigious creators were either lucky enough to have natural momentum in their creative lives, or they made this momentum their priority. The goal after we find good work is to keep working.

In the small acts of daily creativity and the grand career projects, amazing things happen when you keep at things for a sustained period. Small advances add up to large gains, and moving translates into progress. It's why busy people do more, and why prolific people become great. They build a vast body of work lined with the labour of their learning.

Without momentum, life gets in the way of the work you want to do. Distraction is a common affliction. Inertia creeps in. Procrastination, misalignment, inactivity—these are all forces that stop you creating. Sustained production is the best bulwark against these powerful waves of resistance. Regular production gifts momentum.

There is a subtle difference between amateurs and professionals. Professionals produce prolifically. Amateurs do not. To rise from the ranks of the amateurs, you must have work to show the world. Production is the route to becoming the person you want to be. Your production function reveals your preferences. With each new idea you learn, with each new piece created, you forge yourself.

Creative momentum creates a flywheel of production and further engagement. Momentum is required across and within the MEGA phases. It's easy to pick your next problem if you're building on work or skills already developed. If you're already down a rabbit hole, it's easier to go a bit deeper.

Quality from Quantity

To compose a handful of truly spectacular songs, you may need to generate hundreds upon thousands of mediocre tunes. The implicit presupposition here is that you are learning from each new attempt. In the scrap heap of the first one hundred attempts, you discover the elements or styles that will start to work in your next hundred. From vast quantities of work, quality emerges. Many of the great creative figures are known for thin slices of sheer excellence in massive bodies of work. A MEGA practice must culminate in production. It is through production that you crystallise your creativity and contribute to the culture.

Steve Martin says, "Be so good they can't ignore you." Work of a certain standard requires sacrifice; it requires that you become prolific. There is a power in mastering a craft with dogged determination. When you reach a certain level of skill (in thinking, writing, cooking, business-building, or whatever you've chosen), the world opens up and embraces you. People can't get enough—and they will give you their time, their money, and their admiration. Focus on working and producing, and increase the cadence of your output.

Be wary of fake momentum. There is a difference between signal and noise, between light and heat. There are all sorts of sideshows that make you feel busy but don't advance your projects. There are caveats and valid objections to the call for quantity. Quality matters a great deal in creative endeavours, and if we encourage the sharing of less-than-stunning material, do we not litter and foul the world with junk? Do we not lower the standard for good work? There are different replies to this: First, people can produce things and not share them.

We can apply a filter at the Amelioration phase. Second, consider that the space of creative ideas is not limited like our physical world. We can just keep adding things to the global pile, and then mine the outputs for treasure, and thereafter we can push the junk away to the endless edges. Think of a creative graveyard on the margins of Possibility Spaces—no one needs to visit again. This may be the cost of uncovering the abundant genius of someone like Picasso.

It might help to think of fast creativity and slow creativity. Fast creativity is a need for speed—it says you can do more. Fail fast. Learn by doing. Produce. Publish. Contrast this with slow creativity and the benefits of connecting with your craft. Slow creativity is the leisurely wandering process of connecting to your craft—which is more about process than outcome. Slow creativity is about quality and meaning and connection. Fast creativity is a more feverish output in the pursuit of improvement. Sometimes your creativity will be fast, and sometimes it will be slow. You need both modes in your creative life.

In your attempt to become prolific, by regularly releasing your stuff into the wild, you will fail. You'll get bad feedback and suffer cringeworthy mistakes while making inept attempts. You'll be found out in public—and this is precisely why you should do it. Mistakes are the best way to learn. It's only when we idle along—producing nothing, saying nothing, hiding—that we miss out on becoming better. These mistakes—egregious and embarrassing at the time—become harmless debris on the path of the creatively prolific. By becoming prolific, you prioritise momentum and create a haystack of material. Even if you don't find needles, you've created a stack of good hay—and the more you harvest, the more you have.

The effect of producing many works is that your ideas compound on each other. Compounding occurs with consistent production—a wonder of the world. There is an old tale about a wise man who invents the game of chess and presents it at the palace. The emperor is so impressed he offers any reward that the man can name. The man asks for one grain of rice on the first square of the chessboard, doubled on each following square. The emperor agrees— then realises too late that by the sixty-fourth square, the total exceeds all the rice in the kingdom. Investments that are allowed to compound make great fortunes.

In the same way, creative learning and action add up nonlinearly. Radical things are possible at the far side of your production function. Call it the flywheel effect. If you keep momentum, and stay immersed in something long enough, compounding kicks off. But there is a catch: this flywheel is not fed by consistently doing the *same things*. You need to challenge yourself, vary your production, and learn new ideas. In this way, your knowledge and expertise compounds.

Every sketch, riff, draft, or idea adds to your potential energy to create. The myth of overnight success persists because that is all we see from the outside. The breakthroughs don't come from any single effort but rather from the quiet layering of attempts over time. What looks like sudden genius is often the delayed bloom of unseen iterations, the invisible math of compounding creativity. Keep showing up, and your past self keeps paying forward. The best kinds of craft get better the longer you work in them.

Jerry Seinfeld has a saying: "Don't break the chain." He aims to write jokes every single day. Each day that he writes, he puts a big red *X* in the calendar; his goal is to have no days without it, an unbroken chain. This daily commitment to production is what creates momentum in his work and creative life.

Know When to Quit

Bill Watterson is the creator of the wonderful cartoon strip Calvin and Hobbes. *The story of his career is unusual. After a decade of producing perhaps the most popular cartoon in the world, he suddenly decided to retire. Leading up to this, he was offered a $400M licensing deal, major movie projects, merchandise offers. But he held an extraordinary position:* Calvin and Hobbes *was done. He closed the shop and told all the money-grubbers to leave him alone, and he rarely came back into the public eye.*

He said this about his decision: "This isn't as hard to understand as people try to make it. By the end of ten years, I'd said pretty much everything I had come there to say. It's always better to leave the party early. If I had rolled along with the strip's popularity and repeated myself for another five, ten, or twenty years, the people now 'grieving' for Calvin and Hobbes *would be wishing me dead and cursing newspapers for running tedious, ancient strips like mine instead of acquiring fresher, livelier talent. And I'd be agreeing with them. I think some of the reason* Calvin and Hobbes *still finds an audience today is because I chose not to run the wheels off it. I've never regretted stopping when I did."*

I think about the Calvin and Hobbes comics often. My brothers and I loved them as kids. Only someone like Watterson could have written them, someone who respected the quality of their work and knew when to quit.

For myriad reasons, we are attracted to work we've already done, ideas already covered, projects already finished. Old ideas are comfortable. New projects are daunting and demanding, so we are tempted to keep grinding on the old. But we have to start new things so we don't repeat ourselves, and to do this, you must know when to quit.

Quit, stick, finish. You have three options in a creative project: keep working on it, leave it unfinished and work on something else, or finish and share your work. Of course, this is simplified, but the phrase helps keep opportunity cost in mind. You might find another project far more engaging, or learn more, or simply have a higher likelihood of doing something great. This is why in the Amelioration phase, you must think critically about the lifespan of your work and execute accordingly.

If you keep making the same thing because of commercial or social pressure, you'll fall out of love with your craft. Often this will mean sacrificing significant income or prestige to become a beginner in a new field. But if you listen to your motivation and flow states, and the voice that tells you what interests and engages you, the decision is usually easy.

It's also hard to stop doing things that are working well. It's hard to reinvent yourself and change styles or fields. And only you will know when it's time. Your creative life will see death and rebirth, and you will know deep down when you must start something new.

If you are creatively engaged with a project, that is still a good sign, and you should probably keep working on something. But you should regularly ask: Is this the best thing I can be working on? Only you will know when it's right to move on. As always, your project selection depends on the person, the field, and the problem. Annie Duke, in her book *Quit: The Power of Knowing When to Walk Away,* says knowing when to walk away is a valuable skill. The sunk cost fallacy keeps us working at things we should ditch; we can't walk away from the investment of time and energy already made. The creative path requires quitting a lot—but at the right times. Kill a project when it no longer excites you, when you're doing it more for others than yourself, or when there is something much bigger you can work on.

Sometimes a problem is so important you have a moral duty to keep working on it. Imagine if Marie Curie had finished up early in her radioactivity research. Imagine if Fritz Haber had given up on synthetic fertiliser.

You get to decide what you keep momentum on. Although most people should be starting new projects more of the time, I remain a fan of unreasonableness in creative work. When people get obsessed about detail, when they keep working past the point anyone advised—and wonderful things happen. A work may look close to complete to others, but if you think there is more to do, trust yourself. If you remain motivated, and you're able to continue to refine to the nth degree, stay at it and stay enthused. The best reward for good work is more work.

PART 3:
MEGA LIVING

Why creativity matters.

CHAPTER 8:
MANY LIVES

High Agency – Reinvention

Life is not about finding yourself. Life is about creating yourself.

—George Bernard Shaw

Nothing that is allowed by the laws of physics is beyond the scope of human creativity.

—David Deutsch

The science of creativity is still nascent. There is a suspicion that creativity is linked to many of the big questions like consciousness, personal agency, and moral responsibility. In some ways, creativity is what happens between our inputs and action—but this formulation points right back to the mystery of our creative brains. By expanding the space for creativity, we expand the range of decisions we can make and change the course of our lives. Creative thinking gifts us possibility, and this grants us agency.

The figure below shows how your past collapses into your current situation. We are anchored by the past and by forces out of our control, but our futures are liberated by creative agency. At each point, the future is open again with possibility. Many lives lie before us.

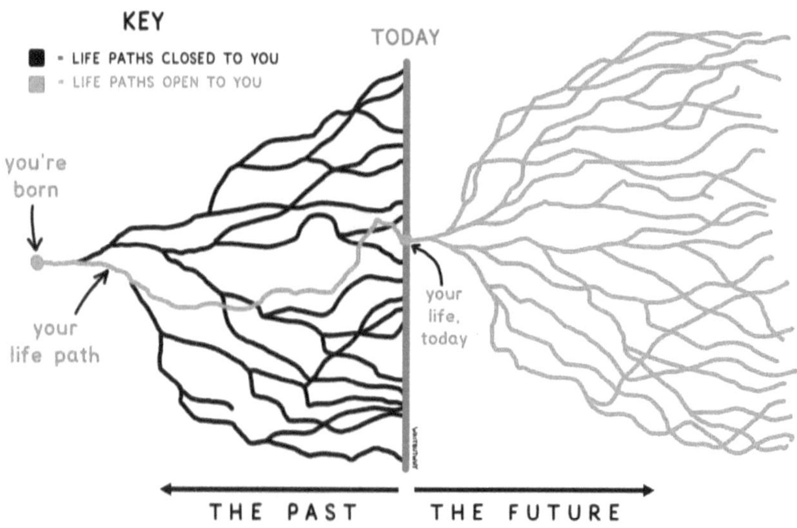

Source: Tim Urban, On X: @waitbutwhy

High Agency

For every decision we face, we have the choice to expand our set of options with more creative solutions. Creativity and agency are intrinsically connected. Agency is an approach to problem-solving that says you can keep putting new solutions on the table indefinitely—you are restricted only by time, energy, and imagination. We never have to accept the default.

In this way, creativity underpins agency. Creativity allows us to see the world not only as it is but also in terms of what is possible. This is a fundamentally optimistic view of human potential. If we are intentional, we can see many life paths, imagine many worlds, and use our creativity to affect the most desirable of the futures. The exploding number of possible options can both inspire and intimidate the creative individual. Agency increases the dimensionality of our thinking, offering us new lives. Highly agentic people see the world and their futures as pregnant with possibility. They see things in higher resolution, becoming optimists because they know that most problems have solutions.

The beauty of agency is that it can be endowed. Just by reading this book, you have been introduced to, or reminded of, your agency. The more you engage with the MEGA steps, the more options you'll find, and the more futures you can see. More exploration offers more ideas. More generation leads to more solutions. In each phase of creativity, you can exercise more agency: in choosing problems, in what you decide to learn, in the variety of solutions you come up with, and in how long you spend honing your work.

There are limits to your agency. Life's not fair. There are things outside your control: where you're born, when you're born, whether you get sick, whether you get lucky. You have to play the hand you're dealt. But even with a bad hand, agency is how you make the best of your constraints. Agency is how you navigate between possible lives. The choices you make impact your future, whether you ultimately had a say or not.

Reinvention

Every day offers an opportunity for new creative engagement. You can work on new things. You can make new friends. You can find new things to care about. You can travel, and learn, and move, and create. Our creativity offers endless opportunity to reinvent ourselves.

It's never too late. Frank McCourt was a schoolteacher his whole life, and at age sixty-six he wrote his beautiful Pulitzer-winning memoir *Angela's Ashes*. Julia Child released her first cookbook at age forty-nine. Vera Wang was a figure skater before she was a journalist, before she entered the fashion world at age forty. Penelope Fitzgerald launched her literary career at age sixty and won the Booker Prize two years later. Wallace Stevens was an insurance executive for most of his life before he became widely appreciated as a poet in his later years.

Psychologists talk about fluid and crystallised intelligence. Fluid thinking is about processing power—how fast you can do calculations and your ability to reason through and solve problems without relying on past knowledge. Researchers believe fluid intelligence declines with age. Crystallised intelligence is much more interesting. Crystallised intelligence is your accumulated knowledge and skills. Very few problems are solved with fluid intelligence. The most interesting and worthwhile problems will invite you to bring your unique crystallised knowledge to the problem. Crystallised knowledge becomes deeper and richer with age—this is wisdom, in a way. Your scope for reinvention expands as you go—you just need to keep looking for problems to apply it to.

Our identities are never fixed because our capacity for creativity keeps us fluid. We can experiment with our days, living many lives, choosing the best of them. You will reinvent yourself at least a handful of times in your life. What you care about when you are twenty years of age might be very different to your preoccupations in late adulthood. As your identity changes, your interests change. Think of your identity in layers. You pick up new interests and discard others. This adding and shedding is how you reinvent yourself. Time spent engaged in something interesting is never time wasted. As you develop your interests, notice how your sense of taste changes. Your knowledge and skills accumulate; thus, as you age your capacity for reinvention and unique insights increases.

CHAPTER 9:
VALUE CREATION

Abundance – What Creativity Does

There is no doubt that creativity is the most important human resource of all. Without creativity, there would be no progress, and we would be forever repeating the same patterns.

—Edward De Bono

Before Jeff Bezos conquered online retail, he was a lover of books. Amazon began as a bookseller. In the early 2000s, they made one of my favourite products in the world: the Kindle. The Kindle started with a simple question: How could reading books become more accessible? That led to the question: What do people value about books? It wasn't the paper or the weight. It was access to ideas and stories—quickly, comfortably, conveniently. Once the team separated the value from the format, a new possibility opened: a book didn't need physical pages to stay meaningful. That reframing was the creative breakthrough. To make it possible, Amazon borrowed a technology from outside publishing—E Ink—which could display text with the soft clarity of print.

From there, the development process became straightforward. Every decision centred on making reading faster, easier, and more accessible: long battery life, instant downloads, and a screen that worked in sunlight. When the Kindle launched, it sold out immediately. The Kindle is a reminder that creativity isn't about novelty for its own sake. It's about creating something of value. We can now carry an entire library in our pockets.

Creativity is called different things in different contexts. It is *imagination* in the arts, *invention* in technology, *insights* in science, *innovation* in business, *ingenuity* in everyday life. Creativity, applied correctly, improves society. Creativity produces value. To get to new knowledge and products, we need the right engagement of motivation, exploration, generation, and amelioration. There is an endless universe of wealth that we might configure. And, as far as we know, it's up to us.

A focus on creativity and value creation calls for a revolution of modern work. If we took the work of motivation seriously, our list of societal challenges and the way we value knowledge and skills could be dramatically altered. We would change the way we explore and learn in organisations and encourage generative and impactful ideation over busywork and performative meeting management. We would implement and ameliorate quickly because that is how we would reward creative work. Our scope of value would also shift to undervalued domains and types of creative work, which would also undermine our recent obsession with material wealth and information technologies. There is a crucial difference between production and productivity. Much of productivity today is simply busyness: unnecessary action unaligned with true motivation. This new kind of productivity often prevents true creative engagement and production. Put aside productivity; it is creative engagement and the creation of value that you seek.

Abundance

There is dazzling scope to make the world better and more beautiful. It's in our hands to inspire each other to do more meaningful and creative things. There are vast tracts of desert we can inhabit and make green. There is ugliness everywhere that we can make less so. Let's not talk about GDP growth and abstract economic terms. Let's talk about gardens where there was once only dirt, about delicious meals on hungry plates, and magnificent inventions that replace tired bodies. Let's talk about the power of art to change minds and influence craft. Creativity, more widely construed, is the route to our collective flourishing. More creativity actualised according to the many passion projects and great work people have in them—that is the way to our thriving. In the same way personal creativity requires a set of conditions for a practice to thrive, our collective creativity requires freedom of speech and pro-creativity societies.

Some people hold the broken view that wealth is a fixed quantity. They feel strongly that there is one finite pie in this world. They fixate on this pie. This pie must be evenly spread between all. Our efforts, they say, must go into slicing and measuring and distributing the pie. But this idea is wrong—worse, it is murderous because it stifles efforts to grow the pie. The current pie is not enough for us all. The way the pie is spread is unfair, and we should improve these inequalities—but if we proceeded with only the current quantities of pie, everyone would eventually go hungry.

Once you understand what creativity is and how it works, you understand that we can make more of the pie, and different types. Creativity is pie-making. Creativity is problem-solving. Creativity is wealth generation. Every time you reconfigure the world in a useful way, you have created wealth. Whether it's a cabin in the woods, an oil painting on a canvas, a new product line in business, a new theory in an academic field, you have added something to the world: you have created wealth. Money is our crude attempt to account for wealth. Printing presses, penicillin, piano concertos, computers, rocket ships—all these things did not seem likely until some sufficiently motivated people broke through. The more we apply our creativity, the more the improbable is brought into the realm of the possible.

The only path to transformative wealth creation is through creativity. We could still be hand-tilling the fields and harvesting with sack and sickle. Instead, we invented the combine harvester and synthetic fertiliser, and famine is now largely eradicated in the world. Abundance creation is a better goal than scarcity management. We have more resources in the universe than we could ever need, but we need creativity to fetch and transform them into useful things.

Economic value is realised with the introduction of new products and industries, the automation of drudgery, an increase in efficiency, a dynamic start-up ecosystem leading innovation and entrepreneurial experiments. There are externalities in any kind of production. The simplistic view that economic growth is good requires nuance about labour conditions, inequality, environmental impact, and the definition of progress. But any associated problems with economic growth require yet more problem-solving, more creativity.

Once creativity makes contact with reality, individuals can reset course based on the manifested impact of their work. We also know that economic creativity is not the only goal; it is an impoverished people who are engineered only for economy—we want musical and artistic creativity too. We want craft and beauty on our streets and in our homes, and we want to understand the world better with scientific creativity.

Since the Enlightenment, individuals have thrived as in no other period in history. In the last few centuries, culture has changed at unprecedented rates. Creativity drives this of course. The science of Newton and Darwin, the technology of Edison and Tesla, the politics of King and Mandela, the music of The Beatles and Brahms. Culture blossomed when we realised the value of creative individuals and enabled them with rights. Human creativity has been around for thousands of years, but only since the scientific and artistic revolutions of the 1500–1700s have we found the conditions for creative thriving. We have seen that creativity needs freedom, and reason, and the scientific method to leave a lasting legacy of change and value creation in the world. As long as our culture does not stifle individual liberty, or lose faith in reason, or find ways to destroy itself with nuclear or biological weapons, our dynamism will persist.

You might ask how advances in AI add value in a human-centric future. Today, we grapple with the cumulative effects of our creative success. Business and technology are becoming synonyms. The tooling of humanity has improved exponentially, changing the way we all live. We are as gods with nuclear weapons, a Hadron Collider, reusable rocket ships, high-yield agriculture, global internet, and supercomputers. New agents in the computer age, progressing through deep learning and feasting on data and energy, are quickly maturing into new forms of intelligence. A Pandora's box lies with the lid open just a fraction, and the light from inside is already blinding.

At this advent of incredible new intelligence, our understanding of creativity has never been more important. We are on the cusp of maybe the most transformational changes in technology in human history. Artificial intelligence has surpassed what we thought machines could do. We gaze in nervous wonder as large language models surpass humans on thinking and reasoning benchmarks. Many feel that the concept of creativity is under threat. I do not. Not yet. While AI technology is a magnificent aid, if we use the MEGA lens we can see that LLM agents are not creative. They are generative and immensely valuable for automated tasks, but they have no goals, no self-directed exploration, and no obvious way to ameliorate their solutions without the taste and guide of their human programmers. These AI models are a new form of cultural technology, astounding and useful—but not yet creative.

What Creativity Does

By now, hopefully you agree with me that creativity, defined as a process that gets us to new ideas that add value, permeates through all the fields of human endeavour. We will always be fascinated by the major fields, distinguished by artistic, scientific, and entrepreneurial creativity. There are countless other forms, from lifestyle creativity to the creativity of invention, but many antecedent ideas can be allocated or traced to the traditional domains.

What Art Does. Let us start with Brian Eno and the most popular form of creativity: artistic creativity. Eno is a difficult man to describe. He is a musician, a writer, and a cultural critic. He is hard to define precisely because he is so creatively prolific and his projects are wide-ranging. For certain compulsively creative people, it becomes difficult to stay in one domain. Eno wrote a book called *What Art Does*. He calls art a kind of *simulation technology*. Art lets us rehearse life without the consequences. It gives us practice in feeling, in noticing, in imagining other worlds. He defines art as "everything you don't have to do." Art creates safe environments for exploring emotions, ideas, and possibilities. It's a kind of thinking: often a nonverbal, intuitive cognition—and it helps us know things we can't always explain.

We can also see art as a cultural evolutionary tool—a way for societies to test new modes of thinking and behaviour. Just as genes evolve biologically, memes (ideas, styles, aesthetics) evolve culturally, and art is their testing ground. Rather than transmitting fixed meanings, art creates contexts that invite multiple interpretations. Eno believes meaning arises from interaction, not imposition. The viewer completes the work.

Whether literature, film, music, or painting, the arts make our lives richer. Good art reminds us that we're alive. Stories and sets and songs and scenes introduce new ways of experiencing the world. Fiction offers empathy, music explores feeling, painting challenges perception. In the post-rational modern world, we often see the arts as a luxury, when they are in fact essential.

What Science Does. At its core, science is a way of constructing and refining explanations that help us understand reality. These models and theories are never final—they're always provisional, always open to revision. Richard Feynman said, "Science is the belief in the ignorance of experts." Its fallibility is also the source of its power. Scientists are never sure about anything and operate on the basis that better information or experiments will update their explanations.

Science is an engine of ever-better explanations, a disciplined way of being curious and chasing truth. It channels human wonder into systematic investigation. Where art explores possibility through stories and feeling, science explores through hypothesis and experiment. Both are forms of inquiry with structure and variation, but science asks: Can we test this? Can we measure it? Is this the best explanation?

We are storytelling creatures prone to narrative fallacies, confirmation bias, illusions, and wishful thinking; science builds protocols—peer review, falsifiability, replication—to guard against self-deception. It is the great cultural tool to capture and refine collective understanding—a shifting foundation for truth. Science is a cumulative, collective, creative act. Despite its reputation for rigidity, science thrives on imagination, paradigm shifts, and leaps of intuition. Every major scientific advance came from a major creative leap.

What Business Does. Good businesses create value for others. The economic system creates incentives for people to be creative and to make things that make people's lives better.

Of course, there are bad businesses. We are still trying to disincentivise businesses that misapply creativity. Some businesses are rent-seekers— capturing value instead of creating it. The mark of a good business is that creativity is applied to the underlying good or service as well as to its methods of commercialising and value creation. There are many negative externalities in our capitalist markets, but the unrivalled benefit of encouraging entrepreneurship is that people are incentivised to be creative where they might not have been. Economic incentives have resulted in wonderful societal gains such as new medicines and new technologies. Business can harness science to create value, and that is a wonderful thing when done honestly and correctly.

Art, science, business, technology—whatever the domain, creativity powers intentional evolution. When creativity works for the good, you see the better angels of our nature. This is not preordained but continuously cultivated. The world you see around you is the result of beautiful and useful new things arising when creative work delivers value. Comedian Dave Chappelle said, "You can't always change the world, but you can make a corner pretty nice."

CHAPTER 10: POTENTIAL

So I'm not going to spend what's left of my life hanging round waiting for it. I'm going to settle for small, random stabs of extreme interestingness—moments of intense awareness of the things I'm about to lose, and of gladness that they exist.

—Helen Garner

Creativity is an expression of aliveness.

—Annie Murphy Paul

Every person is creative. Every field is creative. It is my belief that all thriving individuals require creative engagement. I contend that a creative life is a key component of a good life. It's all about connection to people and craft and ideas, and the secret lies in artful engagement.

Each of us must figure out what to do with our creativity. The great American president Theodore Roosevelt spoke these immortal words about engaging in the creative arena:

> It is not the critic who counts: not the man who points out how the strong man stumbles, or where the doer of deeds could have done them better. The credit belongs to the man who is actually in the arena, whose face is marred by dust and

sweat and blood; who strives valiantly; who errs, who comes short again and again, because there is no effort without error and shortcoming; but who does actually strive to do the deeds; who knows great enthusiasms, the great devotions; who spends himself in a worthy cause; who at the best knows in the end the triumph of high achievement, and who at the worst, if he fails, at least fails while daring greatly, so that his place shall never be with those cold and timid souls who neither know victory nor defeat.

The last part of this book was written in New York City, a good contender for the creative capital of the world. Walking these streets, you feel like the world is alive with possibility. Great feats of engineering tower over you. Creative energy spills out onto the streets: writers in cafés, entrepreneurs in low lofts, scientists gathering for conferences, musicians busking on the streets. That feeling, this potential energy of our creative selves, is what we need to cultivate—wherever we are.

Standing in Central Park, an immense city encircles you. The high-rise buildings are marvels of science and construction, the restaurants carry centuries of cuisine and tradition, the cultural centres house museums and theatres and libraries. People are bustling in the streets with big ideas and business plans and world-changing dreams. Creativity enables all of it—and whether you're in New York or New Delhi, Copenhagen or Cape Town, your creativity matters.

I hope you've found the book helpful. Developing this framework and writing this book has changed me. I look at things differently; I look at people differently. I look at life and culture with a MEGA lens; it makes me ask: What was the creative process behind this? What is the creative potential here? How can creativity be applied to make this better?

Creativity is the golden thread through all our lives. There are other threads, of course: your community, your health, your values. But creativity connects all cultures, fields, and peoples. A philosophy of creativity cannot be separated from a philosophy of living. Creativity infuses life; it is the force that shapes your world in every sphere. Demarcate the domains of living, and you will also see how each part of life bleeds into the others. You will see how more creativity can aid you.

With the MEGA framework, you can see how creative application expands your set of choices. Whether you find the resolve is another question; the path to greater agency is open to you. MEGA living starts by acknowledging that you have untapped creative potential in your life and work. That you can cultivate this creativity for the good with earnest attempts, an open mind, and an optimistic outlook. You'll need to pour your energy into worthwhile things; trust the process of craft and knowledge and mastery, and trust that you will keep finding things that fulfil you.

Creativity researchers differentiate between everyday creativity and radical creativity. I do not see a difference in process. We can bring the same creative attitude to work and life. In quotidian tasks or grand artistic decisions, caring about creativity is the key to elevating ourselves. All of us want to do great work: to make wonderful things and solve hard problems. These pursuits should not prevent you from living well—they are part of living well. Life has no script. Things are what you make of them. Your creativity gives you the ability to write your own story. At each phase of the MEGA process, you will find reasons not to try. There is hard work ahead, but you can always find ways to stay interested. It is worth the struggle. The struggle is the whole point. In creative engagement you will find the fun, flow, and fulfilment that imbues everything you do.

Each morning, at the break of the new day, you should be excited about what lies ahead. What motivates you? Where will you explore? What will you create? From household tasks like cooking and gardening to grand career projects in arts, business, craft, or science; creativity can be wielded to make things wonderful. That is the MEGA approach, that is the power of creativity.

Annie Dillard said, "How you spend your days is, of course, how you spend your life." What a haunting and hopeful sentiment. Each day offers endless possibilities. Each day you encounter dazzling opportunities to live differently. You owe your future self and future generations more—to leave a richer cultural endowment and a better world. Someday you will look back at your life, and you might ask these questions:

Did you pursue worthy problems?

Did you honour curiosity?

Did you opt for discovery?

Were you true to yourself?

Did you wield your creativity well?

Thanks for reading!

I'd like to ask a small favour if you liked this book:
Please give it a quick review on Amazon—it really
helps to share it with more people.

And if you're interested, every Monday I share a short
weekly email newsletter with four ideas—usually one
for each of the MEGA phases.
You can find this at **megacreativity.substack.com**

Or you can find me on X (previously Twitter) at
@MEGA_creativity

ACKNOWLEDGEMENTS

The creative life is so much better when you have people to share it with. I have many people to thank.

To my wonderful wife Samantha: I could not ask for a better or more loving partner. Thanks for all the support: the caring feedback, the good ideas, for weathering my creative storms, and encouraging me during the many hours it took to write this book.

To my parents, I owe an endless debt of care and nurture. My dad, a deeply creative soul, has always inspired me with his vast range of interests and enthusiasm. And my mom, gifted with good taste, made me care about stories and bestowed on me a love of letters.

To my brothers (and Yohan), all musicians, thanks for the jams, games, and the creative times. A special thanks to Francois for the feedback on the delicate early drafts. And thanks to all family, friends, and colleagues who engaged with the project and shared ideas. I hope you saw our many discussions reflected in the book!

Finally, to Matilda. You can't read this yet, but when you do I hope you'll be proud, and I hope you'll choose a life infused with the joy of creativity.

BIBLIOGRAPHY

Bennis, Warren G., and Patricia Ward Biederman. *Organizing Genius: The Secrets of Creative Collaboration*. New York: Basic Books, 1997.

Boden, Margaret A. *The Creative Mind: Myths and Mechanisms*. 2nd ed. London: Routledge, 2004.

Borges, Jorge Luis. *The Library of Babel. In Labyrinths: Selected Stories & Other Writings, edited by Donald A. Yates and James E. Irby.* London: Penguin Classics, 2000. (Original story 1941.)

Burkeman, Oliver. *Four Thousand Weeks: Time Management for Mortals. New York: Farrar, Straus and Giroux, 2021.*

Cameron, Julia. *The Artist's Way: A Spiritual Path to Higher Creativity. New York: Jeremy P. Tarcher/Perigee, 1992.*

Carse, James P. *Finite and Infinite Games: A Vision of Life as Play*. New York: Ballantine Books, 1986.

Csikszentmihalyi, Mihaly. *Creativity: Flow and the Psychology of Discovery and Invention*. New York: HarperCollins, 1996.

Currey, Mason. *Daily Rituals: How Artists Work*. New York: Knopf, 2013.

Deutsch, David. *The Beginning of Infinity: Explanations That Transform the World.* London: Allen Lane, 2011.

Duke, Annie. *Quit: The Power of Knowing When to Walk Away*. New York: Portfolio, 2022.

Dweck, Carol S. *Mindset: The New Psychology of Success*. New York: Random House, 2006.

Eno, Brian. *What Art Does: An Unorthodox Guide to Doing Things Better.* London: Faber & Faber, 2020.

Epstein, David. *Range: Why Generalists Triumph in a Specialized World.* New York: Riverhead Books, 2019.

Gardner, Howard. *Frames of Mind: The Theory of Multiple Intelligences.* New York: Basic Books, 1983.

Greene, Robert. *Mastery.* New York: Viking, 2012.

Koestler, Arthur. *The Act of Creation.* London: Hutchinson, 1964.

Murakami, Haruki. *What I Talk About When I Talk About Running.* Translated by Philip Gabriel. New York: Alfred A. Knopf, 2008.

McGilchrist, Iain. *The Master and His Emissary: The Divided Brain and the Making of the Western World.* New Haven: Yale University Press, 2009.

Pang, Alex Soojung-Kim. *Rest: Why You Get More Done When You Work Less.* New York: Basic Books, 2016.

Pressfield, Steven. *The War of Art: Break Through the Blocks and Win Your Inner Creative Battles.* New York: Warner Books, 2002.

Rubin, Rick. *The Creative Act: A Way of Being.* New York: Penguin Press, 2023.

Sacks, Oliver. *Awakenings. London: Duckworth, 1973.* ———. *The River of Consciousness. New York: Alfred A. Knopf, 2017.*

Stanley, Kenneth O., and Joel Lehman. *Why Greatness Cannot Be Planned: The Myth of the Objective.* Cham: Springer, 2015.